'What a lovely common-sense book! [I  and inspiring examples, all of which ai young people who have a range of comp Each person is unique and if we follow ueu lead, we will be able to design a curriculum that will be right for each one of them. This book is an excellent place to start. Follow Andrew's principles and really personalise their education.'

— *from the Foreword by Dr Penny Lacey, Senior Lecturer in Education at the University of Birmingham and advisor at Castle Wood School, Coventry*

'This is an intellectual triumph that justifies the presence of teachers in the lives of people who were once defined as "ineducable"... [It] is a book full of practice wisdom, not a model of how we ought to do it but vibrant examples of how we could do it if only we could work out what is going on in the lives of complicated people. Andrew Colley's rapport with other professionals and the families of his client group demonstrate how much more can be done with thoughtfully coordinated resources. My enduring impression is of a determined professional focused on his task with a respectful sensitivity to tensions in schools and families coping with everyday, ordinary events. This is not a call for change but encouragement to persist within the parameters we set for ourselves when we insist that education is for everybody in the institutions we provide. It is pragmatism at its productive best – unashamedly giving us permission to do whatever works in the case of every individual whose personalised curriculum is the only way forward.'

— *Robert Orr, author of* My Right to Play: A Child with Complex Needs *and former head of RNIB Rushton Hall School, Northamptonshire, UK*

'Andrew Colley has managed to write an entirely common-sense, non-academic book about a group of young adults who often defy our pre-conceived notions of common sense. This is an uplifting book based on the everyday experiences of a skilled teacher who clearly loves his job and the young people he works with. I highly recommended it.'

— *Peter Imray, freelance trainer and advisor on Special Educational Needs*

'Andrew has written an indispensable guide for teachers and professionals working with and supporting students with profound and multiple learning difficulties. At the start of the book we are introduced to a group of young people. Their likes and dislikes, strengths and needs are described with warmth and respect. Andrew proceeds to take the reader on a journey, as he stands in the young people's shoes and we see the world through their eyes. We are able to fully appreciate that all behaviour has meaning. It is a form of communication and the onus is on us, the professionals, to ascertain what a young person is telling us, so we can respond appropriately and support their learning. Andrew convincingly demonstrates how the learning needs of young people with PMLD can be holistically met through a personalised approach to their education. The aim is to maximise their independence and autonomy, supporting their right to have control over their environment and to enjoy their lives through being engaged in fulfilling activities. Andrew's practical advice and guidance promotes this concept of citizenship, the students being taught and supported to take "their place" in their school and community and to be valued for their contribution.'

— *Janet Leach, Head of Service, Joint Service for Disabled Children, London Borough of Enfield (LBE) and Chair of the Short Breaks Network (SBN)*

Personalised Learning for Young People with Profound and Multiple Learning Difficulties

_of related interest

Using Intensive Interaction with a Person with a Social or Communicative Impairment
Graham Firth and Mark Barber
ISBN 978 1 84905 109 5
eISBN 978 0 85700 291 4

Understanding Intensive Interaction
Context and Concepts for Professionals and Families
Graham Firth, Ruth Berry and Cath Irvine
Foreword by Dave Hewett
ISBN 978 1 84310 982 2
eISBN 978 0 85700 359 1

Finding You Finding Me
Using Intensive Interaction to get in touch with people whose severe learning disabilities are combined with autistic spectrum disorder
Phoebe Caldwell
ISBN 978 1 84310 399 8
eISBN 978 1 84642 239 3

Multisensory Rooms and Environments
Controlled Sensory Experiences for People with Profound and Multiple Disabilities
Susan Fowler
Foreword by Paul Pagliano
ISBN 978 1 84310 462 9
eISBN 978 1 84642 809 8

Personalised Learning for Young People with Profound and Multiple Learning Difficulties

Andrew Colley

Foreword by Dr Penny Lacey

Jessica Kingsley *Publishers*
London and Philadelphia

First published in 2013
by Jessica Kingsley Publishers
116 Pentonville Road
London N1 9JB, UK
and
400 Market Street, Suite 400
Philadelphia, PA 19106, USA

www.jkp.com

Library of Congress Cataloging in Publication Data
Colley, Andrew.
 Personalised learning for young people with profound and multiple learning difficulties / Andrew Colley ; foreword by Dr Penny Lacey.
  pages cm
Includes bibliographical references and index.
ISBN 978-1-84905-367-9 (alk. paper)
1. Learning disabled children--Education. I. Title.
LC4704.C63 2013
371.9--dc23
                          2012049211

British Library Cataloguing in Publication Data
A CIP catalogue record for this book is available from the British Library

ISBN 978 1 84905 367 9
eISBN 978 0 85700 718 6

Printed and bound in Great Britain by Bell and Bain Ltd., Glasgow *for Gillian and Sam*

Contents

Foreword by Dr Penny Lacey   9

ACKNOWLEDGEMENTS   12

1   **Not Just Babysitting**   15
  Daniel   15
  Ben   16
  Ramzi   16
  Alice   17
  Usha   17
  Sammy   18
  Kyle   18
  Labels, definitions and numbers   19
  A Unique Opportunity   27
  Guiding Principles   29

2   **Getting To Know You**   33
  Research   34
  Dialogue   40
  Observation and interaction   46

3   **'He Meant To Do That!'**   53
  'Challenging' behaviour   56
  Extreme behaviours   61
  Spitting   66
  Sexualised behaviours   67

4   **'What Do You Actually Teach Them?'**   68
  What is a curriculum?   69
  What is learning?   70

What is teaching?		76
What is a lesson?		78
Being happy		79
Communication		81
Independence		87
Fresh air and physical exercise		92
Sensory work		93
5	**Environment, Staffing and Timetable**	**95**
	Integration	95
	Groupings	98
	Space	100
	Resources	102
	Décor and wall space	103
	The staff team	106
	The timetable	107
6	**Target-setting and Assessment**	**114**
	Formal targets	117
	Informal or 'living' targets	118
	Stepping stones	120
	Subject-specific targets	120
	Experiential targets	121
	Assessment	124
	Evidence	127
7	**Moving On**	**133**
8	**Edward's Story**	**145**
	A curriculum for Edward	154
	What makes Edward happy?	156
	How can Edward be more independent?	156
	How can we help Edward communicate a little more?	158
	The environment around Edward	158
	References	161
	Index	163

Foreword

What a lovely commonsense book! *Personalised Learning for Young People with Profound and Multiple Learning Difficulties* is full of forthright opinions and inspiring examples, all of which are based on a deep respect for young people who have a range of complex and idiosyncratic needs. The young people introduced in this book are the stars of the 'production'. They come alive on every page so that readers can easily picture the young people who flick paper, spit, smile, enjoy swimming and shut themselves in small cupboards. Readers can come to understand why the young people behave in ways that could be seen as challenging and can perhaps go on to use some of the techniques that are described in the book, for themselves.

It is necessary to understand that the young people who are the subject of this book have profound and multiple learning difficulties, but most do not have profound physical impairments. They are more than capable of moving around, which in some cases can provide challenges for themselves and those around them. For example Ramzi's pica leads to him eating anything and everything which has led to being overweight. His size can be overwhelming, especially when he is upset and hurls himself at people. Not many practitioners have written about this particular group, which makes this book all the more welcome. Educating young people who offer so many challenges is hard and sharing ideas is very important.

Andrew's book covers many aspects of educating pupils with PMLD in schools and colleges and he puts into practice my favourite motto 'start where the young people are, and not where you think they should be, but you can't leave them there'. Looking carefully at the strengths and needs of each young person is vital if the ensuing education is going to fit the learner. Vygotsky's famous Zone of Proximal Development (ZPD) is implicit in Andrew's ways of working. He looks carefully at what the young person can do independently and what he or she can do with support and puts his teaching in the zone between the two. It is a wonderful combination of respecting the young people for who they are and what they can do but gently leading them forwards to greater autonomy and fulfilment. My latest motto is 'trust the learner to show you the way' and Andrew shows us how to do that in a sensitive manner.

This book is not an academic book. There are few references and no explicit analyses of published research. The evidence for Andrew's many interesting points comes from a wealth of professional experience. He has tried ideas out and analysed what happened. He has questioned what usually occurs and come up with reasons why practice should be different. He has developed his own principles, based on his own experience of working with learners who have very complex needs. It is a very personal book and readers have a clear view of what Andrew feels should be an education for young people with profound disabilities.

Interestingly, Andrew's voice is not the only one we hear in the book. I have already mentioned how the learners are the stars, but there are several other people who are quoted, some at length. Readers learn from a range of experts including a solicitor's firm, a further education teacher, an Intensive Interaction practitioner and a parent. These different perspectives add value to the book by providing material that Andrew cannot.

Personalising the learning for young people with profound learning difficulties is essential if they are to learn anything that has relevance to them. You can't take any pre-written list of attainments and apply them to the individual learners in this book.

Each person is unique and if we follow their lead, we will be able to design a curriculum and teaching approaches that will be right for each one of them. This book is an excellent place to start. Follow Andrew's principles and really personalise their education.

Dr Penny Lacey
Senior Lecturer in Education at the University of Birmingham and advisor
at Castle Wood School, Coventry, UK

Acknowledgements

My thanks are due to the following schools in the UK where I have been able to learn so much about teaching young people with complex needs: The Edith Borthwick School, Bocking, Essex; and Granta School, Linton, Cambridgeshire.

I am also grateful to Hillside Special School, Sudbury, Suffolk, and Southview Special School, Witham, Essex.

Thanks to the following practitioners who provided so much valuable information about practice in their countries: Dr Mark Barber, Consultant in Profound Intellectual Disability and Severe Communication Impairment, Melbourne, Australia; Susan Cassidy, Speech-Language Pathologist, Queensland, Australia; Dr Sheridan Forster, Centre for Developmental Disability Health, Monash University, Victoria, Australia; Erica Green, Advisory Teacher Alternative and Augmentative Communication and Physical Impairment, Queensland, Australia; Kieron Hubrick and Faye Philp, Carlson School for Cerebral Palsy, Auckland, New Zealand; Mimi Kong, Jockey Club Sarah Roe School, Hong Kong; Melissa Larson, Educational Director, The Caroline School at Easter Seals of Greater Houston, Texas, USA; Ann Mudie, Patricia Avenue School, Hamilton, New Zealand.

Also thanks to everyone who helped with this book in so many ways, especially: Julie Abo, Sally Adams, Ann Baker, Jane Barbrook, Dany Barone, Gail Baxter, Dawn Bennett, Paul and Lesley Bird, Helen Bladen, Ian Boatman, Becky Broughall, Michelle Burke, Sammie Byrne, Lucie Calow, Lisa Cambridge, John Carswell, Rosemary Crossley, Leanne Deas, Ruth Dobbs, Chris and Sheree Don, Catherine Drew, Sue Farr, Clare Gormley,

Cathi Howell, Dr Benson Ikuesan, Caroline Ilott, Peter Imray, Kyla Johnson, Dr Penny Lacey, Janet Leach, Shelley Lockwood, Mandy Maass, Toni Newby, Beth Plimmer, Carolyn Prince, Naomi Rezzani, Kirsty Soanes, Katie Taylor, Jo Tighe, Maxine Tyler, Fiona Walsh, Toby Wigmore, Tim Williams, and Annie Aris and Patrick Jacobs of *The Laughter Specialists*.

I owe a special debt of gratitude to Ros Ward, former Deputy Head at The Edith Borthwick School, for the support and advice she gave me when I began working with young people with complex needs.

Chapter 1

Not Just Babysitting

This is a book about as many as 65,000 young people currently in UK schools and colleges, maybe more than 130,000 in the USA, and similar numbers too in schools in Australia and Canada. There will also almost certainly be many more out in the community who don't access education at all.

Here are just a few of them. We'll be getting to know each of them a lot better throughout this book.

Daniel

Daniel is 17. He is quite a capable young man and can read a few words in very simple books if his teacher points to them carefully or says them to him first. He can trace his name and other words and is able to pick letters and words out on a computer keyboard. He can speak, but only a very few words and then very quietly. Words like 'tea' which he likes and 'toilet' where he often seeks refuge. He can understand instructions consisting of two or three parts quite well. Above all, though, Daniel is very anxious all the time. So anxious in fact that he will not mix with any of his peers and only occasionally with his teachers. When he is especially anxious he will hurt himself. He will bang his head as hard as he can on the walls, bite his hands and punch himself. He also bites other people. Students and teachers. Not harmless little nips, but proper bites which draw blood and need medical treatment. Sometimes he will throw chairs, tables, crockery around the room.

Ben

Ben is 16. He is tall and strong. He doesn't speak, though recently he has started wagging his finger and saying a word which sounds like 'no'. He understands some simple instructions, but forgets them quickly. He can hold a paint brush or a fork, but only with great difficulty. Usually he throws them away. He tries very hard to make the Makaton signs for 'B', as in 'Ben', 'swimming', and 'minibus'. He smiles a lot and makes loud high-pitched screaming noises. He loves the company of other people and particularly adults. He shows this by running up to them and hitting them as hard as he can, or spitting in their face, or biting them, or grabbing their clothes, or blowing mucus down his nose into his hand and giving it to them. His favourite way of gaining attention is to pinch the flabby underside of someone's arm as hard as he can. He will do this to friends, teachers, his family or complete strangers. He has no sense of danger. If left to his own devices he would just as happily walk down the middle of the road as on the pavement. When he is particularly excited he might throw a chair, or a plate, or a cup. He loves going out on the bus but often hits the window so hard that he cracks it. Ben has a wheelchair, although he is perfectly able to move around without it. He is strapped into his chair sometimes for his own and others' safety, though, at school at least, this is not encouraged.

Ramzi

Ramzi is 18. He's a big boy and enjoys eating. He suffers with a condition called 'pica' which means he is liable to eat anything he can reach: grass, leaves, flowers, papers, plastic. His own faeces. He weighs over 300lbs. Ramzi doesn't have any recognisable spoken language, though he does have a vocabulary of several 'words' of his own. He enjoys chatting to people in his language. He is quite good at following instructions, even relatively complex ones, when he is motivated. He laughs a great deal, sometimes on his own and sometimes with others. Perhaps because of his size, he likes nothing better than going to the seaside or the pool and swimming about or just floating in the water. He can spend hours doing this. Apart from swimming, Ramzi isn't really very motivated to do much. He is quite happy to spend all day lying on a beanbag or in the garden. If he thinks someone is trying to get him to do something he would rather not do, he can get very angry. He will spit at his teachers and family, or sometimes hurl himself at them, pressing them against a wall or knocking them over. Often, though, his anger is directed at himself and he has big raised welts on his hands from where he has bitten them so hard for so many years.

Alice

Alice is 19. Her spine used to be so curved that she couldn't sit or stand up. Most of the time she spent curled up on the floor. However, she has now had an operation to insert two rods in her back and she is seeing the world from a standing position for the first time in her life. She struggles to keep her head and eyes still, but really enjoys holding a book or being read to by her favourite people. She is very thin and her arms and legs seem fragile. Alice doesn't speak, but seems to understand some simple instructions. She is often in great pain, especially from mouth ulcers, and cannot really control the production of saliva in her mouth. When she is uncomfortable she screams loudly and bangs her head very hard with her hands. She enjoys the fresh air but doesn't like being too hot or too cold. She is quite independent and can go to the fridge and take a yoghurt, though she needs help eating it. Sometimes she shuts herself in a small cupboard. Just to get away from things.

Usha

Usha is 16. She always seems so happy, though this may be because she has Angelman syndrome, and one of the features of this is that the person appears to be smiling. She loves hiding things from you. Usha doesn't have any language and apart from her quiet laughter and very occasional cry of distress she makes no sound. She can follow the odd simple instruction. She loves being with people. She reaches out to them, hugs them. Usha cannot walk and is usually in a wheelchair. She does have a walking frame and likes setting off around the room, but usually sinks to the floor after a few steps. She also loves crawling around the floor and pulling herself up on a chair. Usha likes putting things in her mouth. Especially pieces of soft plastic. She has to be watched carefully and occasionally her teacher has had to call an ambulance because she has started choking on something she has swallowed.

Sammy

Sammy is 18 and has Down's syndrome. He used to speak a little when he was younger but now makes no recognisable sounds at all. He can follow two- or three-part instructions quite well. He is also a very happy person and likes making people laugh, often by burping loudly or hiding things under his clothes. On one occasion, one of his helpers lost her mobile phone. She rang it to find out where it was. It was down the front of Sammy's trousers. Sammy is a very tactile person. He loves the feel of his own and other's skin. He loves creeping up behind friends and teachers and slipping his hand up inside their shirts. He can hold a pen or brush quite well but struggles to get the marks on the paper. Though he does love drawing on things. On anything in fact: the table, the chairs, himself, other people. Sammy has his own small house which he shares with two carers, one of whom is his older brother. He loves turning on his music or the TV.

Kyle

Kyle is 16, and is very laid back. He can spend hours just flicking through a magazine. Not reading it. Not even looking at the pictures. Just flicking and enjoying the sound it makes, or the flickering of the pages in the light, or the feel of it against his skin. Like Ramzi, Kyle doesn't talk but does have his own language. He really enjoys people talking to him in his language. This makes him smile. Kyle's dad is a musician, and so he loves listening to rhythms and music. He loves experimenting with a keyboard, or music software. He is quite independent and will perform fairly complex tasks to get something he wants: like a drink of squash or a cup of tea. He will also lead a helper towards something if he can't get it for himself. What he doesn't like is walking about very much, particularly on uneven ground or up and down stairs. He's getting better at this, but it still makes him very nervous.

Labels, definitions and numbers

Depending on where they happen to live in the world, young people such as Kyle and Usha and the others can be described as having Profound and Multiple Learning Difficulties (PMLD), Profound Intellectual and Multiple Disability, Multiple Impairment, Complex Learning Difficulties and Disabilities, Severe and Profound Disabilities, or simply Complex Needs. These are all labels which have or will be attached to Sammy, and Daniel, and Alice and their classmates, and hundreds of thousands of others. Often, the words 'with autism' or 'with epilepsy' are attached, so that Kyle, for instance, is described as having 'PMLD with autism'.

The labels come and go, move in and out of fashion, are adopted in one country or fall out of use in another. It's not the labels that matter particularly, because they can describe people who walk and talk, those who don't, those who have very complex physical needs and require high-tech chairs, those able to manage some of their personal needs, such as toileting, and those who can't and never will. It also includes those whose behaviour presents no problems at all to their teachers or their family, and those for whom behaviour is the most challenging issue they will face.

I have changed most of their names, but Ben, Alice, Ramzi, Usha, Daniel, Sammy, Kyle, and a few of their friends we will meet later on, are all real people. I have described them as I have found them. I haven't invented anything or anybody. I didn't want to create a composite or 'typical' person with PMLD, because there isn't such a thing. Nor is there such a thing as a 'typical' person with autism, or a 'typical' person with Down's syndrome. You will have read that Sammy for instance does have Down's syndrome, and maybe guessed that Ramzi and Kyle are autistic. We will look briefly at these and other conditions in Chapter 2, but I don't want to get too bogged down in definitions or syndromes. This is not a book about medical conditions, or psychology, or genetics or biology. It's a book about teaching and learning.

Even in the UK, there is no one agreed definition of the term currently in favour: 'profound and multiple learning difficulties'. Here are just a few of the definitions in current practice. London-based Douglas Silas Solicitors, who specialise exclusively in education and disability and particularly in cases concerning special educational needs, acknowledge the problems defining the term:

> *There is no accepted definition of profound and multiple learning disabilities, but it is commonly associated with pronounced developmental delay with significant physical and sensory impairments and epilepsy.*
>
> *Most people with profound and multiple disabilities will have physical disabilities and will be unable to walk and have to use a wheelchair. They may have hearing and sight problems. They will communicate non-verbally, that is, they will not speak or if they do, will use only a few words. Some may use signs and symbols or look and point to what they want. Some of the main characteristics are:*
>
> - *difficulties with reading, writing and comprehension*
> - *inability to understand and retain basic mathematical skills and concepts*
> - *limited vocabulary and communication skills*
> - *short attention span*
> - *under-developed co-ordination skills*
> - *lack of logical reasoning*
> - *inability to transfer and apply skills to different situations*
> - *difficulty remembering what has been taught.*
>
> (Douglas Silas Solicitors 2012)

These definitions put an emphasis on physical disabilities, but don't address the often challenging behaviours young people display.

The PMLD Network, which is chaired by the charity Mencap, suggests the following, which does include reference to behaviour:

People with profound and multiple learning disabilities:

- *have more than one disability*
- *have a profound learning disability*
- *have great difficulty communicating*
- *need high levels of support*
- *may have additional sensory or physical disabilities, complex health needs or mental health difficulties*
- *may have behaviours that challenge us.*

(PMLD Network definition (short version) 2004, published by Mencap)

It is also possible to try to define PMLD in terms of IQ, as in this from the organisation About Learning Disabilities:

One can categorise learning disabilities into four very basic groups – mild, moderate, severe and profound. Intellectual impairment based on IQ scores is one way to categorise a learning disability:

- *50–70 – Mild*
- *35–50 – Moderate*
- *20–35 – Severe*
- *less than 20 – Profound.*

As aforementioned, an IQ score is not sufficient in wholly defining the level of learning disability. This is because IQ scores can fluctuate due to personal development and growth.

(About Learning Disabilities 2012)

This definition also acknowledges the inadequacy of categorising people with profound learning difficulties solely on IQ score. Behaviour, disability and environment will of course affect any IQ testing even more than it would with people who do not have learning difficulties, and IQ scores alone are rarely used these days in any educational context as the only way of assessing someone's ability or potential. The IQ is a fluid thing and can increase or decrease over the course of a lifetime dependent on a range of environmental, personal or social conditions.

Peter Imray is a trainer and adviser in special needs education and worked for many years at The Bridge School, Islington, London, which has been consistently rated by the Office for Standards in Education (Ofsted) as 'outstanding'. He states that young people with PMLD:

- *are pre-verbal in terms of intent*
- *may communicate for needs and wants only*
- *are totally physically reliant on others (for their safety)*
- *have significant difficulty with understanding abstract concepts*
- *have a limited understanding of cause and effect.*

(Imray 2005)

Peter also talks about these young people's 'profound egocentrism'. This is an important term, perhaps one of the keys to understanding everyone categorised as having profound and multiple learning difficulties.

Profound egocentrism in this context is about being the absolute centre of your own world and expecting to be at the absolute centre of everyone else's. It's about being aware only of your immediate needs and no one else's. Ben for instance, like all of his peers to a greater or lesser extent, has absolutely no concept of when or where it is appropriate to seek someone's attention. If he sees a teacher who he wants to spend some time with, he will simply launch himself across the room towards them, knocking aside tables and chairs until he gets to them. He wants to be with them, and that's all that matters at that moment. We'll see more examples of extreme egocentrism in Chapter 3.

From an educational perspective, it is possible to go some way to defining PMLD in terms of The UK National Curriculum 'P-Levels'. The P-Levels (or scales) are a set of descriptors used in the UK and some other English-speaking countries for recording the achievement of pupils with special educational needs who have not yet reached the first level of the National Curriculum (Level 1). These scales are split into eight different levels with P1 being the lowest and P8 the highest.

The performance descriptions for P1 to P3 outline the types and range of general performance that some pupils with profound learning difficulties might characteristically demonstrate, and it is useful at this point to include them here (see Box).

National Curriculum P-Levels

P1(i) Pupils encounter activities and experiences. They may be passive or resistant. They may show simple reflex responses. Any participation is fully prompted.

P1(ii) Pupils show emerging awareness of activities and experiences. They may have periods when they appear alert and ready to focus their attention on certain people, events, objects or parts of objects. They may give intermittent reactions.

P2(i) Pupils begin to respond consistently to familiar people, events and objects. They react to new activities and experiences. They begin to show interest in people, events and objects. They accept and engage in coactive exploration.

P2(ii) Pupils begin to be proactive in their interactions. They communicate consistent preferences and affective responses. They recognise familiar people, events and objects. They perform actions, often by trial and improvement, and they remember learned responses over short periods of time. They cooperate with shared exploration and supported participation.

P3(i) Pupils begin to communicate intentionally. They seek attention through eye contact, gesture or action. They request events or activities. They participate in shared activities with less support. They sustain concentration for short periods. They explore materials in increasingly complex ways. They observe the results of their own actions with interest. They remember learned responses over more extended periods.

P3(ii) Pupils use emerging conventional communication. They greet known people and may initiate interactions and activities. They can remember learned responses over increasing periods of time and may anticipate known events. They may respond to options and choices with actions or gestures. They actively explore objects and events for more extended periods. They apply potential solutions systematically to problems.

(Qualifications and Curriculum Authority 2009)

A lot of students with PMLD function at or around P-Levels 1–3, but not all. Some of their achievements can be categorised as, say, P2, but others – in listening for instance – might be somewhere within P4, or even higher. It's not an exact science. Daniel for example has a reading ability which in some areas can be recorded as high as P5, but his acute anxiety and often violent behaviour makes it difficult to record this progress at all in other areas.

A definition which is expressed sometimes is that people with Profound and Multiple Learning Difficulties are 'like babies'. And by extension, I have heard it said that teaching students with PMLD is 'like babysitting'. This is not accurate or helpful. Defining young people in their teens and beyond in terms of milestones normally applied to infant development can only ever be partially correct. Of course, they have some elements of behaviour which could in some circumstances be described as 'baby-like': toileting, extreme egocentrism, difficulties feeding themselves, etc., but they are not babies. Daniel, Ramzi and their peers are 16, 17, some even older.

They have life experiences, quite complex feelings, hormones. In some cases they are nearly 6ft tall and extremely strong. They are in fact very nearly grownups. We should never ignore this, and describing them as 'like babies' should not be used as an excuse to just 'babysit' them.

Even teachers – quite understandably really given the extreme challenges of teaching a PMLD group – can grab hold of strategies, even whole curricula which have been designed for early years, for 'babies', and try to apply them to their older PMLD classes. This is rarely appropriate. To quote Peter Imray again:

> Of course there are (developmentally) some similarities between young neuro typical (NT) children and those with severe learning difficulties, but to simply import a curriculum designed for young NT children cannot and indeed must not be the answer. What happens is what has tended to happen with variations of the (UK) National Curriculum, those with SLD can sometimes (even often) get so far but no further, because progress is assumed to be conventional and linear – in other words neuro typical – and because teaching (and therefore learning) has been compartmentalised into subject areas.
>
> (Imray 2011)

With the possible exception of the 'just babysitting' model, all the attempts at definitions quoted above are helpful to a greater or lesser degree and certainly most of the young people featured at the beginning of this chapter fit into most of these definitions. More or less.

Definitions can attract funding, help when placing young people in classes, or groups, or residential settings, and assist in planning lessons and activities. But in fact what we have around the world is a growing population of young people with very complex needs – starkly unique and individual young people who deserve to have those unique and individualised needs met.

Right at the beginning of this chapter, I quoted some figures for numbers of young people with complex needs in the UK and other countries. It's actually extremely difficult, though, to arrive at accurate figures, mainly because terms and categories vary wildly. For the UK for instance, in the 2001 *Valuing People* report, the Department of Health estimated that 65,000 children had severe or profound learning disabilities, although gave no age range for the word 'children' (DoH 2001). On the other hand, the October 2012 statistical analysis by the Department for Education covering primary, state-funded secondary and special schools puts 10,255 school age children in the 'PMLD' category, 29,935 in the 'severe learning difficulty' category and a further 970 in a 'multi-sensory impairment' category, giving a total of just over 41,160, a figure which shows an increase of 2000 from the first statistical analysis of this type carried out in 2009 (2012).

For the academic year 2008/09, the US National Center for Education Statistics gave a figure of 130,000 people aged 3–21 with 'multiple disabilities' enrolled in public (state) school programmes. Statistics drawn up by the Australian Institute of Health and Welfare (2008) identified an incidence of about 351,000 people of all ages having a severe or profound intellectual disability, but does not break that figure down further into ages.

There may also be many more young people who are simply kept at home or in care and are not included in any official figures. The picture becomes even more blurred once people get beyond school leaving age.

However many there are, though, all of them are so much more than just a category, more than the sum of their most memorable or obvious behaviours, more than their officially diagnosed conditions, their IQ or current P-Level.

Like all of us, they have complex and changing personalities. They have strengths and weaknesses, likes and dislikes, things they do and things they don't do. Good and bad habits. They are each as much a product of their upbringing, parents, financial and social circumstances and life experiences as they are of the conditions and syndromes they were born with or acquired in their early lives. Like all of us, their lives are unfinished narratives: organic and ever-changing according to circumstance, environment and experience.

So this book is not about syndromes or conditions, categories or diagnoses. It is a book about teaching and learning.

Because when I tell people about Ben, and Alice, and Ramzi, and Usha and the rest of the young people in my classes, I seem to be often asked this question: '*What do you actually teach them?*' It's a reasonable question. A bit tiresome sometimes, but understandable.

It's particularly understandable in the context of the education systems that are perceived – rightly or wrongly – as being based on tests and exams, results and league tables. Linear, target-driven systems which prioritise measurable outcomes. Systems aimed for the most part at a 'model' pupil who works systematically through a number of levels to reach – or not – a predictable outcome. But as we will see, Alice, Ramzi, Daniel and the rest don't learn in that way. They learn, they progress, they develop, but it is not always possible to measure their achievements in a linear pattern, let alone set them targets which we hope they will one day reach, especially in relatively academic areas such as 'reading' or 'number'. They may well 'plateau' at different times in their lives, but again this should not be an excuse to stop teaching them. A plateau is usually just a place to rest; maybe pitch camp for a couple of days, before the next stage of a journey.

A Unique Opportunity

So in a way this book is an answer to that question: '*What do we actually teach them?*' It is a book about how to educate each of the young people described at the beginning of this chapter, and maybe also the hundreds of thousands of others around the world.

We have a unique opportunity to create truly personal and exciting school and college experiences for these young people. It is not the case that in the UK for instance we are obliged to teach young people with complex needs according to some rigid and prescriptive National Curriculum in pre-set subject areas, and particularly not when they reach the age of 16. In fact, as teachers, we have a lot of freedom to create a curriculum on a school-by-school, or even student-by-student, basis as long as it is 'broad and balanced'.

Yes, as these quotes from the Qualifications and Curriculum Authority emphasise, each child up to age 16 has a right to be offered the '*full range of subjects of the National Curriculum*', but there are '*no nationally specified times for particular subjects. It is for schools to determine, and justify, the amount of time allocated to different parts of the curriculum.*' In fact when planning a curriculum in the UK even for children with learning difficulties between the ages of 5 and 16 the aims and values in the National Curriculum provide simply '*a starting point for discussion*'. Above all, schools '*should take account of their school aims and the needs of the pupils attending the school (which will change as they progress and grow older)*'. Within the National Curriculum Guidance for England and Wales there is also a specific acknowledgement that 'the range of therapeutic needs and paramedical care is wide. Provision for these needs is a legitimate and essential element of the curriculum and should be planned for.' Even out-of-class time is recognised as '*contributing to aspects of learning that are important for pupils with learning difficulties*' (QCA 2009).

Elsewhere, the Qualifications and Curriculum Development Agency made it clear that '*the starting point for your planning lies with the learner rather than in any existing programmes or accreditation routes*' (QCDA 2007).

The picture in other English-speaking countries is similar. Teachers in New Zealand have considerable freedom with regard to the content of the curriculum as long as they reference the '5 Key Competences' of the mainstream curriculum: Thinking; Using Language, Symbols and Text; Managing Self; Relating to Others; and Participating and Contributing. In Australia, a mainstream national curriculum has recently been introduced, with a 'pre-foundation' curriculum expected to follow which will cover PMLD students. Teachers of these students currently have freedom in deciding what to teach. In the United States, where educational provision is decided at state level, most special needs teachers have freedom to determine their own curriculum.

There can never be one overriding pedagogy or curriculum which will fit the seven young people described at the beginning of this chapter, let alone the hundreds of thousands of others around the globe, because the young people we are talking about are as diverse as any of us. We all learn and grow in different ways, and so do they.

Guiding Principles

Aspects of many existing methodologies are of course relevant, for example process-based learning, intensive interaction, total communication, problem solving, and community awareness. All of these will be discussed later in this book.

More important perhaps are certain key principles which underpin teaching and learning. These key principles include but are not limited to the following:

- Young people with profound and multiple learning difficulties have the right to have their development and learning needs met on a personalised basis.

- Young people with PMLD have the right to be treated as individuals and to become as autonomous as is possible within their personal circumstances.

- Teaching methods reflect the fact that young people with PMLD do not necessarily learn and develop in a linear or hierarchical way. Learning may be unpredictable, unexpected or tangential.

- All teaching, assessment, target-setting, etc. must take as its starting point the individual student.

- Teaching and learning methods must be multi-disciplinary and multi-agency. Teaching must be holistic, to reflect the complex needs and abilities of each student.

- Teaching and learning cannot be hurried. All learners must be given the time and space to engage, respond and communicate.

- Learners in the 14–25 age range have specific needs which cannot necessarily be addressed using off-the-shelf curricula for younger neuro-typical children.

- Where possible, behaviour is seen as communication or self-expression. Challenging behaviour is treated as a response to anxiety or stress. Appropriate behaviour is always acknowledged and disruptive behaviour often ignored.

- The physical, social and emotional environment around the student is central to establishing good teaching and learning. Outdoor and physical activities play a key role in learning and development.

- It is recognised that working with young people with PMLD can be extremely stressful both physically and emotionally. The welfare and well-being of the teaching team is central to the development of a successful learning environment.

The principles outlined above are at the heart of this book, but other principles, excellent in their own right, need to be tempered with the hard steel of reality. Compromised even. For instance, the principle that including young people with complex needs systematically with their more academically able peers is actually a very complex and open-ended issue, and will be discussed more fully in Chapter 5.

Earlier on in this chapter, I said that just like all of us, the lives of young people with the most complex needs are unfinished narratives.

During our lives, we all, more or less, create our own narrative. The story of our lives. It's an unfinished story, but a story nevertheless, with many unpredictable twists and turns. Many joys and sorrows. Many successes and failures.

Young people with PMLD don't often get the chance to do that. For practical reasons, they tend to be 'done to'. They are defined, analysed, restricted, contained, prescribed, followed and led. This book accepts the inevitability of much of that, but also tries to find ways in which these young people can be helped to create and define their own lives.

It's about starting from the point of view of seeing them *as they are*, and not as we expect, or have been told they are. That's the least we can do for them.

In particular, this book is about educating people with PMLD from about age 14 onwards. An age when behaviour, size and emotional development combine to make the application of a more traditional curriculum even more difficult.

Daniel, and Ramzi, and Ben will never go to university, they will never have a career, or even a job. They may never have their own home, yet the content of a traditional 'mainstream' curriculum often presupposes all these outcomes: the maths we need to do, the history we need to know, the languages we need to speak. From that flow certain conventions to do with teaching styles, lesson planning, etc. We will be challenging some of these conventions in Chapter 4.

However many people with complex needs there are around the world, they will all be supported in one way or another for the rest of their lives. That isn't to condemn them, to see them as lesser people. It's about being realistic. It's about being absolutely frank about what they each need and why. Because 'supported' doesn't mean 'dependent'. In the same way, later in this book we will see that 'integration' isn't the opposite of 'segregation'.

What will make them happy and fulfilled? How will they communicate? What is their potential for autonomy, and what help will they need to achieve this?

We can and should be able to put in place a programme of learning which prepares each and every one of these young people to fulfil their potential, to be ready for the future, to be comfortable with themselves, to be 'at home in their own skin', in the same way that any good education system does.

Our willingness to care for each of these people, to have hope for them, to look after them is what marks us out as human, as civilised. But do we go far enough?

Later on in the book, we will ask how we can build learning programmes on a truly individualised basis which as far as possible recognise these students as young adults with a desire for autonomy, well-being and self-expression like everyone else, but at the same time acknowledge their profound and multiple learning difficulties.

In Chapter 2, we will begin the journey of creating relevant and appropriate school and college experiences for these young people by looking at how we can get to know each student. Not just their names and ages, their syndrome or diagnosis, but really get to know them as unique and changing individuals. Just like all of us.

Chapter 2

Getting To Know You

Getting to know the young people we are working with is the first step. It is the foundation on which we as teachers and practitioners will build a curriculum for each of them in school or college.

There is no rule about how long it will take to get to know each of our students before we start 'actually teaching' them. That's because the process of getting to know is open-ended. It will go on for as long as we have responsibility for them in a class or group. The short pen portraits of Kyle, and Ben, and Ramzi and their friends at the beginning of this book are no more than sketches, a moment in time. By now they will have moved on. Ramzi might not spit so much. Alice's mouth ulcers may have cleared up. Usha may have stopped using her walking frame altogether. Sammy may have stopped putting mobile phones down the front of his trousers.

There will never be a point when we can say that we truly know everything about a young person with complex needs. As we will see in Chapter 4, just as each young person is constantly changing and developing, so the curriculum around them must be constantly changing and developing too. However, we do have the freedom to devote the first weeks or months of each year to getting to know each one as well as we can. This will allow us at least to begin the process of creating a personalised curriculum.

For the purpose of this chapter I'm going to divide the 'getting to know' stage into three non-consecutive parts: research, dialogue and observation/interaction. 'Non-consecutive' because there is a great deal of overlap between all three, and nor do they have to be taken in any particular order. As with so many aspects of working with young people with complex needs, it's an organic process.

Research

Usually, the young people we work with come to us with some kind of stated diagnosis or condition. The profiles of some of the young people I have met reveal the following terms: Angelman syndrome, cerebral palsy, craniosynostosis, Down's syndrome, Duchenne muscular dystrophy, global developmental delay, neuronal migration disorder, Prader-Willi syndrome, Rett syndrome, Worster-Drought syndrome. Young people with severe autism, or autistic spectrum disorder, are also now commonly placed in groups of students with profound learning difficulties, especially if they have multiple needs or additional sensory or motor impairments, or if their autism has a profound effect on their learning.

The list above is not exhaustive, nor is it generally possible just to define a young person in terms of one condition. Hardly any young people with complex needs have one neat diagnosis attached to them. Some may have several named conditions, each affecting them in different ways.

Many have coexistent conditions which would not normally be expected to impact on their learning and development, but do require medical intervention. Of these, epilepsy is common amongst young people with complex needs. It is frequently the coexistent condition which needs most urgent medical intervention, especially if it is severe and life threatening. As we will see in Chapter 8, it is often this medical condition which parents focus on in the early years of their child's development and not the diagnosis – autism for instance – which might have greater impact on their learning.

It's a complex picture, and as I have already said in Chapter 1, this is not a book about 'conditions' or 'syndromes', it is a book about teaching and learning. Nevertheless, it is important for a teacher to have some knowledge of any diagnoses their students have, especially as they may impact on their learning, or require significant skills, expertise and training of staff.

So here in alphabetical order are very brief definitions of some of the conditions teachers may come across in their professional practice. I make no claim to being an expert on any of them, and would recommend anyone reading this book to conduct their own research and talk to professionals in the field to find out for themselves about these and other diagnoses.

Where possible I have included a link to websites which will give much more information about each one. I have tried to reference the websites of some of the major charitable or support networks for each condition or syndrome in the UK, Australia and America.

Angelman syndrome

Angelman syndrome is a chromosome disorder which causes severe learning difficulties. Consistent characteristics of Angelman syndrome include: developmental delay, speech impairment, and movement or balance disorder. People with the syndrome often appear to have a happy demeanour, are easily excitable and have a short attention span. Those affected will require care throughout their lives.

For further information: www.angelmanuk.org; www.angelman syndrome.org; www.angelman.org.

Autism and autism spectrum disorder

Autism is a lifelong developmental disability that affects how a person communicates with and relates to other people and to the world around them. It is a spectrum condition, which means that it affects people in different ways. For people with autism the world can seem to be a confusion of sounds, sights, textures, etc., and this can lead to very high levels of anxiety, and often associated behavioural issues. Some people with autism have accompanying learning difficulties.

For further information: www.autism.org.uk; www.autism-society.org; www.autismspectrum.org.au.

Cerebral palsy

Cerebral palsy is a condition which affects muscle control, movement and posture. Some people have cerebral palsy so mildly that it is hardly noticeable, while others will require care for the rest of their lives. Associated conditions can include learning difficulties, epilepsy, communication issues, problems with eating and toileting, and occasionally behaviour issues.

For further information: www.scope.org.uk; www.cerebralpalsy.org; www.cpaustralia.com.au.

Craniosynostosis

Craniosynostosis is a condition which causes changes in the growth pattern of the skull in infancy. This can result in abnormal head shape or facial features. The impact on the developing brain can lead to visual impairment, respiratory problems and in some cases to learning difficulties.

For further information: www.craniosynostosis.net; www.cranio facial.com.au.

Down's syndrome

Down's syndrome (also known as Down syndrome) is caused by the presence of an extra chromosome in a baby's cells. It occurs at conception and is irreversible. People with the syndrome experience delays in their development and will often have a degree of learning difficulty, ranging from very mild to severe. Children with Down's syndrome may experience difficulties with speech and communication.

For further information: www.downs-syndrome.org.uk; www.ndss.org; www.dsawa.asn.au.

Duchenne muscular dystrophy

Duchenne muscular dystrophy is a genetic condition caused by a mutation in the genetic code. Although primarily a neuromuscular condition affecting movement, muscle tone and balance, in some cases the effect of the condition on the brain can lead to learning difficulties or behavioural issues.

For further information: www.muscular-dystrophy.org; www.mdaustralia.org.au.

Global developmental delay

Global developmental delay is a general term used to describe a condition that occurs during the developmental period of a child between birth and 18 years. It is usually defined by the child being diagnosed with having a lower intellectual functioning than what is perceived as 'normal'. It is sometimes accompanied by significant limitations in communication and learning, and can give rise to behavioural issues.

Neuronal migration disorders

Neuronal migration disorders are a group of birth defects caused by the abnormal migration of neurons in the developing brain and nervous system. This can result in structurally abnormal or missing areas of the brain. Symptoms vary but often feature poor muscle tone and motor function, seizures, developmental delays, learning difficulties, and problems with eating.

For further information: www.ninds.nih.gov.

Prader-Willi syndrome

Prader-Willi syndrome is a genetic disorder which is present from birth. People with Prader-Willi syndrome may exhibit developmental delay, learning difficulties and challenging behaviours. One of the more consistent characteristics of the condition is an insatiable appetite and almost constant feelings of hunger.

For further information: www.pwsa.co.uk; www.pwsausa.org; www.pws.org.au.

Rett syndrome

Rett syndrome is a neurological disorder that is thought to be caused by a genetic change, although is not considered to be hereditary. It usually affects only females. Although it is present at birth, it is not usually detected until regression occurs at about one year of age when skills are gradually lost. People affected by Rett syndrome are severely physically disabled and have profound learning difficulties. Rett syndrome is often accompanied by epilepsy, curvature of the spine or scoliosis, loss of speech, and eating and drinking difficulties. Children with Rett syndrome often display repetitive hand movements such as wringing, patting and crossing fingers.

For further information: www.rettuk.org; www.rettsyndrome. org; www.aussierett.org.au.

Worster-Drought syndrome

Worster-Drought syndrome is a form of cerebral palsy that affects the muscles around the mouth and throat. This can cause problems with swallowing, eating, talking, etc. People with Worster-Drought syndrome sometimes have additional difficulties with coordination, learning and behaviour. Epilepsy is also present in some people with Worster-Drought syndrome.

For further information: www.wdssg.org.uk.

As I said before, this list is not exhaustive. Every practitioner, teacher, parent or carer reading this book will be able to add more terms.

The research phase will also include taking the time to read through all the appropriate files and documents which will have accompanied each young person probably since they were very young babies. Once a child with complex needs reaches the age of about 14, there will most likely be a mass of paperwork including any or all of the following and more:

- Admission documents
- Report cards
- Records of achievement
- Profiles
- Statements of educational need
- Annual or periodic reviews
- Individual education plans
- Speech and language assessments
- Occupational therapy and/or physiotherapy assessments
- Sensory assessments
- Behaviour management plans
- Incident reports
- Academic assessments against national or state criteria
- Mobility plans
- Reports from social services
- Feeding plans
- Body maps
- Medical reports and assessments
- Respite reports
- Personal care files.

The documents each child has will depend on past history as well as which country, state or school provision they are currently in.

Each and every piece of information may help in the ongoing process of creating a truly personalised curriculum.

It may not be appropriate for a teacher or other professional to read certain documents, however, especially where they might concern legal issues, past trauma, difficulties at home and other sensitive areas. A significant number of young people with complex needs have difficult home lives, and it is often not appropriate or necessary for class teachers, support workers or teaching assistants to have access to this information, except where trauma at home might have a significant impact on the student's behaviour, their ability to learn or their welfare. It can easily be forgotten when working with a young person with profound and multiple difficulties, whom we may know relatively intimately in many ways, that they too have a right to privacy. Just like you or I, their lives are their own, and we must never forget that.

Indicators of academic achievement are of course vital. National Curriculum P-Levels used in the UK and elsewhere, individualised report cards, national standards and information gained from state standardised tests all provide essential information about the young person's ability and progress, although normally only within a linear pattern predicated on the expected progress of neuro-typical children of a similar age.

However, for a young person with complex needs academic achievement can only ever be one part of a very complicated and constantly changing picture of where they are at any one time. As already stated in Chapter 1, Kyle's, and Ramzi's and Usha's abilities will typically progress, plateau or regress for short periods in an unpredictable pattern. A curriculum based only on academic achievement can never really respond to the unique and personal needs and learning style of a young person with complex needs.

Dialogue

Setting up an ongoing dialogue with the people who know them best is an essential step when preparing to work with any young person with complex needs. This will include professionals such as speech and language therapists, occupational therapists and physiotherapists.

Before we begin working with the young person, as well as in the early weeks spent together, the key people to talk to will be previous class teachers, support staff, and parents or carers.

If Usha for instance was about to come up to a new class, the past and future teams around her may need to discuss some or all of the following:

- What are her current preferred communication methods? Does she use any forms of Augmentative and Alternative Communication (AAC)?

- Does she use any assistive technologies to support communication, self-expression or independence?

- What has she enjoyed or not enjoyed doing over the last year or so?

- What does the new class team need to know to ensure her safety?

- To what extent is she aware of danger, both in the classroom and in the community?

- What are her current targets, both formal and informal?

- What are her relationships like with her peers, and in particular with any young people who may be progressing to the next class with her?

- How has the teacher made provision for her mobility and posture issues in the set-up of the class?

- How has the staff team managed any behaviour issues?

- Are there any cues she commonly displays which might indicate an approaching seizure or a change in behaviour?

- Are there any special arrangements made for eating?

- How has the class team managed her personal care?

- Are there any other medical issues not flagged up already in existing reports or care plans?

- Has the staff team had to have any special training to deal with any medical or care issues such as epilepsy?

- Are there any times of the day when she seems more or less responsive or engaged?

- How does she get to school and are there any ongoing issues with transport?

- Is there any cultural or religious observance which needs to be built into her school day? If these are important at home or their community, then they should also be part of school life for that person as well.

It will be important to find out whether dialogue with the young person's parents or carers is generally easy and effective. On one level this will be simply if parents or carers have a preferred method of communication: for example e-mail, phone, home/ school book, face to face.

Maintaining a clear and effective channel of communication with home or respite care is one of the most important things a teacher can do on behalf of a young person in their care. But it isn't always easy, of course. The parents of a young person with complex needs are no different from all parents the world over. Some embrace their child's schooling enthusiastically – occasionally too enthusiastically – some are happy to stay away and only get involved at formal events such as parent/teacher consultation evenings, some prefer to have no contact at all, and a few are openly hostile to the school environment.

What is undeniable, though, is that the parents are the ones who know the young person like no one else ever will. They have been there from the start. They have suffered the same joys and pain as all parents and the particularly challenging experience of coming to terms with having a child with complex needs. They have suffered levels of anxiety and confusion, guilt and despair, joy and hope that for most of us are unimaginable. They have shed more tears than they will care to remember. They are probably exhausted and drained from years of worry. They may not have slept properly for more than a couple of nights in a row since their child was born. They have spent endless hours in meetings, consultations and on the phone with doctors, social workers, therapists and teachers; and as Edward's dad says so poignantly in Chapter 8, they may have come to realise that even consultants are not gods. No one really has the answer to all their questions.

We should never forget the experience of the parents and carers of the young people we teach. It is hard sending a child off to school, but most of us get used to it and build it seamlessly into our lives. When our child is exceptionally vulnerable, though, the fear of harm, or of the unexpected phone call from school, will be all the more acute.

Communication with parents should be sensitive and non-judgemental, even when they are challenging or criticising us. We must talk to them, but above all, we must listen. Listen with an open heart and mind. Often, in their stressful lives, that is all they need. We may find out that the young person is very different at home from at school. Maybe she is more independent, maybe less.

Like all parents, though, they may give mixed messages. They may over- or underestimate their child's abilities. Some accept very easily the realities of their child's difficulties; others will never accept. Some of them may be confrontational and demanding; some will be constantly kind and generous. Some will be anxious, and some will appear cool and laid back. We may come to see these characteristics reflected in their son or daughter, because as I have said before, a young person with complex needs is so much more than their particular diagnosis or condition. Like all of us, the influence of their parents is an important contributor to their development as people.

One of the most important questions we as teachers can ask the parents of a young person we are just getting to know is very simple: '*What do you want for your child?*' The answer to that question can be short and to the point, it can be long and emotionally charged, but in my experience there are three things which stand out and are usually part of most answers in one way or another. Parents or carers want their child to be happy, to be able to communicate a bit more, and to be as independent as possible. It is actually what we all want for our children. What we want for ourselves really.

Happiness, communication and independence: these three things should be at the heart of any curriculum for young people with complex needs. We'll be looking in detail in Chapter 4 at whether happiness can be taught and modelled, how communication skills can be developed, and at ways to foster independence and autonomy as part of a personalised curriculum.

There is a fourth wish of course, and it is implicit in the parents' desire for their son or daughter to be more independent: they would like their child to be able to have more independent toileting skills. In the 'getting to know' phase it's important to have clear and up-to-date knowledge of the personal care needs of the young person, so that we can do our best to build on that and take it to the next level of independence.

Getting a clear picture of a young person's personal care needs and abilities isn't always easy. By its very nature, it is a private and intimate process. It takes place behind closed doors and although ideally the child should have a regular 'personal care partner' who they know and feel comfortable with, the hectic reality of school and college life means that often different people may be involved, sometimes in the course of any one day.

The situation may also be very different at home where routine can be less important and rigid than it often is at school when carers and teaching assistants will usually have to cope with the reality of having to undertake personal care for a number of young people in a limited amount of time.

Personal care is part of a personalised curriculum. It isn't an add-on. It's not something that gets in the way or needs to be fitted round lessons. For most of the young people we are getting to know here, there will be issues around personal care for the rest of their lives. In terms of their education, it's as relevant as their next school lesson. That's not to say that the aim of personal care is always to 'teach' the young person to use the toilet independently. Many will never achieve this. But the processes involved in personal care, especially those involving communication and trust, are opportunities to build positive experiences and 'learning' into the young person's life.

Appropriate personal care can only really work as part of a fully cooperative process between all parties involved in the care of the young person, and especially between home and school. This starts with the discreet sharing of knowledge and experience among all those involved.

To be effective for the young person at school, all the knowledge you build up about a child needs to be kept in some accessible format and shared where appropriate with everyone who is likely to come into contact with them for any significant amount of time in school. This will include not only teachers, teaching assistants, mid-day assistants and therapists, but also replacement or cover staff, who may only come in for a day or two, but still need to be as informed as possible about each young person in their care.

Realistically, the vast amount of paperwork, reports and assessments accompanying each child through his or her school life will be kept for safety and convenience in lockable files in a secure environment. Some of that material will be confidential, and some not directly of relevance to the teaching and learning process with that child. However, brief summaries of important information to support the young person's learning and daily routine can be kept in the classroom and, at the discretion of the teacher, be available to anyone coming into significant contact with the class.

A class file for Sammy, for instance, might include some or all of the following:

- a photo
- Sammy's age and/or date of birth
- a short pen portrait describing what he is like as a person, his likes and dislikes, etc.
- whether or not he has any spoken language and whether he uses any alternative or augmentative communication

- a brief statement of his medical needs, including information about where to access specialist support

- a brief outline of personal care needs, including the name of his 'personal care partner' if he has one

- a note about break and lunchtime arrangements, including any specialist eating

- behaviour issues, including where to access further information about behaviour management

- things we are encouraging Sammy to do or discouraging him from.

These files should contain the minimum information we would expect anyone coming into a PMLD classroom for the first time to know. The first thing a replacement teacher, or new teaching or mid-day assistant, should do when they come into a class is to sit down in a quiet corner somewhere and read through the class file.

Observation and interaction

Young people like Sammy and Ramzi and Alice may have spent their whole lives being closely monitored and controlled. Almost from the moment it was first noticed that they may be developing in different ways from others, which in some cases – Ben's or Alice's for instance – might have been the day they were born, they may have been prodded and poked, watched and analysed. Out in the community or at family gatherings, they might have been kept on a tight rein – sometimes literally. If they have severe epilepsy, like Edward who we are going to meet in Chapter 8, they may have been followed closely by someone carrying a mysterious bag for their every waking – and sleeping – moment.

Because in the main they can't speak for themselves, our own and others' perception of them can have become defined by what others say about them, or because of something written down in a report or assessment. How much has their behaviour been defined by expressions such as 'He does that', 'He never...', 'She always...', 'Autistic children can't...'?

This is not to devalue the research and dialogue phases of the process. It's just that a report or assessment can never be the final word, in the same way that a label such as 'autistic' is just that: a label. It's a convenient word and not the whole complex, changing and often wonderful picture of a young person with complex needs.

We saw in Chapter 1 that in most English-speaking countries there is no nationally prescribed curriculum for young people with profound and multiple learning difficulties. There is not in the main an obligation to follow a rigid subject-based programme of study, even in a diluted form. This means that we have the opportunity of building a truly personalised curriculum for each young person in our care. What it also means is that we have the opportunity, possibly unique in educational practice, of being able to spend significant time with the young person without the pressure to actually 'teach' anything. We can just be with each one of them, on their terms. Observing, yes, but not in a clinical way. In a different way maybe from how they have been observed before. Not analysing. Not looking for anything. Just watching, sitting, sharing.

Ideally, of course, this observation should start before a young person actually comes to your class. Let's imagine for instance that Ben is about to progress to the next phase of his schooling and is going to move class. Appropriate opportunities should be set up to allow the new class teacher and other key members of the staff team to spend time with him in the class he is leaving. With no particular agenda, it is an opportunity just to get to know him within a classroom environment, support him in some activities, and chat to teaching assistants and other staff working with him.

Following on from this, he can come over to his new class for an hour or so, or a morning, or maybe a whole day. First with a member of staff from his existing class and then later perhaps just being brought over and left with the new class team.

Then, when the school year starts, and Ben is officially in your class, try to maintain this period of getting to know, this time of curiosity, for as long as possible, for the benefit of you and your team as much as for him. Try to avoid sticking to a rigid timetable, keep assessments and targets to a minimum, allow him to explore his new environment as freely as possible, sampling different places, groupings, resources and experiences, working with different people each day.

A colleague and I were lucky enough once to find ourselves on our own in the classroom for about an hour towards the beginning of the year with a young man called Karl. Diagnosed as autistic, he has no spoken language. He was by reputation a 'difficult' student, who when anxious could bite himself and others, head-butt people, empty cupboards onto the floor, or jump over fences and run away. Because of these behaviours, he was very closely monitored by staff.

So we decided to take a risk. We unlocked the cupboards and put as many of the resources as possible out on tables. I told Karl that he could do whatever he wanted. Then we sat down next to him, and waited.

At first, he was anxious. He grabbed me. Pushed his forehead hard against the side of my head. I tried not to react. Just to sit. Just to accept him as he was. He hit himself a few times – on the thighs. Nothing too hard. I said, as gently as possible, 'Don't do that Karl. You'll hurt yourself.'

He got up and paced up and down, moving further and further away from us each time, but always coming back and sitting with us again, grabbing my colleague, forcing his head against hers. He began to explore some of the games and other resources we had put out. Some of them he sniffed, some of them he licked or put in his mouth, some he threw on the floor. This went on for a long time – 20 minutes maybe. Only when we thought he might be in any danger – from swallowing a small object for instance – did we intervene, and then only with as light a touch as possible.

Eventually he opened the cupboard where we kept art equipment – paint bottles, brushes, pens, pencils, crayons. This was normally locked and out of bounds because of Sammy's and Ben's tendency to paint themselves, their teachers and everything else in sight.

Karl started moving backwards and forwards in front of the cupboard, getting closer and closer each time, occasionally biting his hand or jumping up and down on the spot, but gradually getting used to having access to this normally secret place.

He grabbed a tray of crayons, walked around the room with it a few times, then sat at a table. He began exploring the crayons, turning them in his hands, smelling, licking, patting, looking. It had taken him about 45 minutes to reach this point.

We put a sheet of paper on the table in front of him. He tore a strip off it and put it in his mouth. He did this several times. Tearing strips off and either chewing them or discarding them.

We put another sheet of paper in front of him. He picked up several crayons one at a time: licking, tasting, exploring. Then he began scribbling on the paper: nothing particular, nothing miraculous, not the work of an autistic-savant. Just scribbles: some round shapes, some long thin shapes, a couple of different colours. He sat at the table and drew for over five minutes. It had taken an hour of more or less letting him be, an hour of 'being with', an hour of cupboards emptied, bins upturned, and the odd bruise, but it had been worth it. We had learnt that Karl would, could, focus on an activity for a significant amount of time. We weren't about to insist he spend every day in the art room, but maybe, just maybe, art and drawing might be something he could focus on with a degree of independence, something he would get praise and encouragement for, something which would make him happy. Something perhaps we would include in his personalised curriculum.

We had learnt something about Karl.

Sharing it with the class team was vital, of course. In fact, informal sharing of things we have seen, learnt or done with each young person is important in the early days with a new class. Have a weekly meeting, or a daily meeting, or whatever suits your way of working, and just share. Jot down things about each young person. Things you have seen. Things you have shared. Above all, things they have done with a degree of autonomy. Don't write them up in tablets of stone, don't keep them on file. Just have them to hand as you get to know the students. Probably a lot of the notes will turn out to be irrelevant, but as you begin to focus on what you are 'actually going to teach' Karl, that rough note about his scribbles on paper might just turn into something more important.

As this period of observation and interaction, this time not so much of teaching, but of 'being with', reaches a temporary conclusion, we will have learnt a great deal about each of the young people we will be working with. Above all, though, we have begun to see each one as they are. There is no need to impose a ready-made, off-the-peg curriculum, because each young person contains within him his own unique curriculum.

Daniel doesn't just like tea, he likes it hot and sweet, and turns to it when he feels he is beginning to get anxious. It calms him down, and he's never thrown a full cup. Just empty ones. So perhaps there's nothing wrong with him being encouraged to make his own cup of tea – with support of course – whenever he wants one. At breaks, during lessons, whatever. He is 17 after all. It's a life skill he will always need.

There's a good reason why Ben tries to make the Makaton sign for swimming. He loves it. He particularly loves being out of his depth, in the deep end, with water wings and floats and supported by two staff, just splashing around, using his whole body. And his behaviour is so much better after a good half an hour in the pool. Maybe we should try to take him swimming every morning?

Ramzi lies down a lot. On beanbags. On sofas. On the floor. It's not surprising really for a boy as big as he is. He must be very uncomfortable most of the time. The weight issue is a complex and a long-term one. We'll need to take a multi-agency approach on that. Parents, doctor, dietitian and respite carers. So while that's going on, why not accept that he likes lying down? Perhaps he actually needs to lie down for his own comfort? So instead of always insisting he sits at a table to work, maybe sometimes – just sometimes – we could get a puzzle, or a simple abacus game – something he has enjoyed in the past – and lie down next to him? Take up his position rather than always insisting he takes up ours, and work together.

When Alice shuts herself in the cupboard, perhaps she is telling us something? Perhaps she doesn't like Sammy's laughing and burping or Ben's high-pitched screaming. She's a 19-year-old young woman after all. And also, the act of getting herself into the cupboard isn't necessarily a negative thing. It's an act of incredible will and autonomy. Left to her own devices, she will drag a chair and a large beanbag to one side, pull open the door which is quite stiff, then go to the fridge, open the door, take a yoghurt, go into the cupboard, make herself comfortable, sit down and shut the door. How wonderful, and independent, and 19-year-old-girl-like is that! There's a lot more to Alice than we first thought. OK, she forgot the spoon for the yoghurt, but then how used is she to getting her own cutlery? Perhaps we have been doing a bit too much for her. Perhaps the spoon thing can be her next target?

Why is Usha sinking to the floor and using her walking frame less and less? Is she getting weaker? Is she getting lazy? Is it no longer fit for purpose? Does she have regular physio? Perhaps this should be a priority for her? Or perhaps she prefers hauling herself round the room by holding on to the furniture? Is there actually anything wrong with that? Perhaps the answer is to rearrange the room to make it a bit more Usha-friendly?

Sammy and Kyle both seem to have very sensory approaches to things. Sammy loves the feel of human skin, though clearly he needs to be discouraged from touching other people's when it's inappropriate. Kyle can sit by the window for hours on end holding a magazine or a catalogue near to his face and flicking through the pages. What's that about? Perhaps Sammy can learn to explore other textures – rough, smooth, anything? Perhaps that can be a short-term target: to explore new textures? Is it significant that Kyle sits by the window to flick through magazines? Perhaps it is not so much the magazine itself he likes, but the play of light. There's another girl in the group who loves light effects too. Perhaps they could work together once a week in the sensory room, exploring light and shadow? They are both quite solitary. Might it be of benefit to both to work together for a while?

If there are 12 students in your group, maybe what they need is 12 curricula?

Before we address that, though, in Chapter 4, we need to look at the first thing you may notice about some of your students: their behaviour.

Chapter 3

'He Meant To Do That!'

Whether we have complex needs or not, behaviour – good or bad – is the way we respond to our environment through language and action.

The form that behaviour takes is dictated by who we are and where we come from. Our life journey up to that point, if you like. Under normal, everyday conditions, our behaviour is an acceptable part of the way we are. Some people like our behaviour and become our friends. Others don't and move on. That's just the way life is.

Most young people with complex needs behave under normal circumstances in ways which to the outsider may seem odd, but are an acceptable and inevitable part of who they are. Daniel speaks very quietly, wanders up and down a bit and likes to spend time on his own. Ben rushes about a lot, and grabs things and people. Ramzi eats a great deal, lies down a lot and hates wearing shoes. Alice waggles her head about, grinds her teeth and likes lying underneath tables. Usha smiles a lot, is very curious, and likes putting things in her mouth. Sammy laughs most of the time, especially at his own burps, and loves touching other people's skin. Kyle rarely makes eye contact, flicks magazines in front of his face, likes sitting down, and doesn't like walking.

Many of these behaviours will simply be a function of each person's condition and may be exacerbated or reduced by how they are feeling, external circumstances or recent history. Others will be a result of their upbringing or the culture of behaviour they live in. All families impose behavioural modes on their children. This is just one of the reasons why all children grow up to be different. A girl or boy with complex needs has been through just the same process. It's why each of them, and each of us, is unique.

This is how each of this particular group of young people behaves normally and it's more than likely that these or behaviours like them will be part and parcel of who they are, off and on, for the rest of their lives. It's what they do, and 'modifying' most of these behaviours is not really what a personalised education should be about.

I remember once proudly outlining to Kyle's mother all the ideas I had for encouraging him to make eye contact with people. I was sure my ideas would 'work' and was equally sure that she would be delighted with my efforts. In fact, she said this: '*Why do you want him to make eye contact? That's how he is. Is it really that important?*'

I couldn't answer. I couldn't think of a single reason why it might be worth spending time encouraging her son to make eye contact. Every reason I could think of had absolutely no relevance to who her son was now or was likely to be in the future. I agreed to drop the whole idea and concentrate on things which would help Kyle grow and develop in ways which suited him. In the grand scheme of things, eye contact came just too far down the list.

Of course, some of these young people's behaviours may be dangerous: Usha putting things in her mouth for instance. Others may be socially inappropriate: Sammy touching people's skin for example. In these cases we can and should be taking steps to help them either to modify their behaviours, or more importantly to be kept safe from danger.

For Usha we should make sure that potentially dangerous items are out of reach rather than trying to impede her oral approach to the world. Even in Sammy's case, we have to respect the fact that he interprets the world to a certain extent through touch and that his preference is for smooth skin-like textures.

Should he touch a stranger in a way that would conventionally be said to be 'inappropriate', at least part of the response must involve explaining to that person that Sammy means no harm. It's what he does.

To a very great extent, it is up to us and to the society around a young person with complex needs to adapt to these behaviours, rather than the other way round. This is how we should start to personalise our response to these kinds of behaviours. As far as possible by accepting them just as they are. Non-judgementally. Above all, we should try where appropriate not to view young people's everyday behaviours through the prism of our own social and cultural conditioning.

Supermarkets are always a good test of this. I was once in a large supermarket with a young man with complex needs. It was just before Christmas and the shop was very busy. We were in the Christmas cake and mince pie aisle. He sat down. Right in the middle of the aisle amongst all the shoppers.

My first instinct was to try to make him stand up. Why? Because sitting down in a supermarket is something people just don't do. Especially when it's busy. I've never done it and I've never seen anyone else do it, so why should he? I tried all sorts of ways to get him up: persuasion, firm words, kindness, bribery, manual handling. But he was almost as big as me and nothing was working.

One of the ladies who stacks the shelves passed by. *'Don't worry about it,'* she said, *'he's not doing any harm.'* And she was right. He wasn't doing any harm to anyone. He was just sitting down. The other shoppers simply walked round him.

I realised that I had never seen a sign in a supermarket anywhere saying you can't sit on the floor. So I left him to it. In fact I sat next to him. Eventually, when he was ready, he got up and wandered off. And so did I. It felt like the most normal thing in the world.

Another boy I know jumps up and down a lot. Very high. Especially when he is happy. He does it in supermarkets. He's actually the only person I have ever seen jumping up and down in a supermarket. People look, of course. Some smile. No one has ever complained. I don't do it with him, though. I leave this one to him!

Behaviour is also usually communication. Certainly in the two supermarket examples, this is true. The boy who sat down was probably tired and communicated that by sitting down. He didn't have a more appropriate means of communication at his disposal. The boy who bounces up and down does it, I think, to communicate his happiness. After all, supermarkets are wonderfully colourful and exciting places.

Neither of these two boys will probably ever understand the complex social rules which tend to prohibit sitting down or bouncing up and down in supermarkets. And why should they? In any case, they are not really rules at all, just tacit agreements among most supermarket shoppers.

Who cares about this unconventional supermarket behaviour anyway? In my experience, people out in the community are effortlessly tolerant, understanding and kind.

'Challenging' behaviour

So far in this chapter we have looked at what we could call normal, everyday behaviour. Normal, everyday behaviour for Kyle, and Ramzi, and all the others. The patterns of behaviour, tics and rituals, vocalisations, verbal and physical particularities which mark each of our young people out as themselves. Behaviour which in general causes no one any harm.

Accepting these behaviours is part of the personalisation process. It's a personal behavioural curriculum if you like. Rather than saying to Kyle, and Ramzi, and Ben and the others: 'This is how I behave, I'd like you to do the same please,' we are saying: 'OK. I accept that this is you. What you do, however odd it may seem to others, causes no one any harm. So just carry on and we'll deal with any consequences. Together.'

Some young people with complex needs also display what is often called 'challenging' behaviour. It's a good term because it's more about the person being challenged than the person doing the challenging. If I feel challenged by the behaviour of someone near me, perhaps it is up to me to change rather than them? It might be a lot easier, rather than setting up a challenge to their challenge, and so on, until someone gets hurt.

Challenging behaviour can take many forms. Sometimes it is not even very challenging at all. Just a bit awkward and disruptive to day-to-day life. More disruptive than sitting down in the supermarket, though.

Often these types of behaviours are characterised by refusal or non-cooperation. Karl, who we met in Chapter 2 exploring the art cupboard, often challenges us by refusing to do things: leaving school at the end of the day, or leaving a room in order to go to his next class for instance.

These are just the sort of minor examples of challenging behaviour which if dealt with in a heavy-handed way can escalate into something much more serious.

One morning Karl refuses to get out of the car at the school gates. This is unusual behaviour for Karl. He has never refused to come into school before. His escort and his driver are circling round, clearly getting anxious and unable to get Karl to move. One option would be to send for people who are specially trained in one of the approved manual handling techniques. They could hold Karl in a safe and not too invasive restraint and walk or perhaps even carry him into school. This may make Karl upset and even more challenging for the rest of the day, but at least he'll be in school.

This approach to conflict resolution takes many forms and should be backed up by thorough training, risk assessments and legal protocols. Resorting to physical intervention is usually absolutely the very last resort and only used when the safety of the young person or those around him is directly threatened.

There is another way, though. Much more time-consuming, but ultimately one which puts Karl himself at the centre of the decision-making process. A method which doesn't compromise his independence or risk upsetting him even more.

First, try to find out why Karl isn't getting out of the car. It won't make him move, but it will help those around Karl to understand him. As it turns out, in this case, he had spent the night before with his dad, who he gets on very well with, and so perhaps it's not surprising that going to school is not top of his agenda at the moment.

Then ask yourself the questions: 'Does he actually have to get out of the car now at this moment? What's the worst thing that would happen if he doesn't?' It turns out that neither the driver nor the escort have to be anywhere in a hurry. Their presence may be making Karl more stressed, especially as they are pacing up and down. So suggest they go off for a coffee. So now there is no real time pressure. No reason to force Karl in any way. Certainly no need for physical intervention.

Is it more important that Karl attends his first lesson, or that he makes his own decision to leave the car, and arrives at school in a calm state? In a personalised curriculum, what matters is managing his response and not the school timetable.

So from now on you have to trust Karl to act independently, maturely even, despite his very complex needs. It's a gamble, but the odds are stacked in his favour, and yours. Don't forget Peter Imray's definition from Chapter 1: people with complex needs are *extremely egocentric*. It's what has got Karl into this situation and it is what will get him out, or more importantly it is how he will get himself out.

If Karl wasn't so extremely egocentric he may have got out of the car by now because that is what his teacher has told him to do. But he is egocentric, so he is staying in the car because that may be the only remaining link with his wonderful weekend with dad. That's all he cares about right now.

You could even acknowledge this by getting in the car with him and just sitting there for a while. He might not want you to of course, so be prepared to get a chair and sit on the path. Sooner or later Karl will make a decision, and it will be his decision. And like a lot of the decisions we all make, it will be based largely on instinct and a sense of self.

Later, maybe five minutes later, maybe an hour later, Karl may decide that staying in the car has its disadvantages. There's no food or drink for instance. There's nothing much to do. School might seem a more attractive prospect with its sights and sounds, and familiar faces.

So just like the boy in the supermarket, he will probably get up and wander into school when he is ready. He may not be particularly happy, but at least he may be at ease with himself. He will have acted independently, and he will have communicated a little of how it feels to have to leave his dad in the morning. Above all, the solution to the problem will have been personal and unique to him. He will have received lots of positive reinforcement for his actions, and just possibly this might make the next incident easier to resolve.

Here's a simple list of strategies worth trying in situations characterised by non-cooperation:

- Give plenty of warning of what is about to happen, especially if it means a change of location.

- Ask yourself if the young person really needs to do what you want him to do.

- Ask yourself if he really needs to do it now, or if it can wait.

- Ask yourself a hard question: is it actually me who wants to move, go to the next aisle, leave the shop?

- Ask yourself: what's the worst thing that can happen if he doesn't do it right now?

- Tell him you'll come back in, say, five minutes and ask him again.

- Go to where he is. Do what he is doing. Sit next to him, lie down next to him. Just be with him. Wait till you feel the moment is right. Then suggest you both move.

- Praise every tiny movement. If, say, Ramzi is lying down and won't get up, as soon as he moves, even slightly, acknowledge it and tell him how good he is.

- Try a different tone of voice, a different volume, a different pace. A different pitch.

- If none of that works, ask someone else to try. A slightly different approach will often work. There's never any shame in admitting you have failed and calling on someone else.

Above all, though, accept that young people with complex needs take time to do things. They do things at a different pace, in a different way, and that's fine. That's who they are. It comes back to how you structure the timetable and the day. If there's no time for the students to react at their pace, then perhaps the timetable, even the curriculum, is too prescriptive.

A young man with autism for instance may need to perform a number of small rituals before leaving one place and going to another: touching things, stamping on things, walking round things. Try to make sure time is built into your activities for him to make his own way at his pace, and on his terms.

Sometimes, changing the environment slightly around the young reluctant person can help. I once couldn't get a boy to leave a pet shop. I couldn't work out what was going on. He was frozen to the spot near a large fish tank. I tried everything, all of the above. It was getting late. I was beginning to run out of reasons why it was OK for him to still be there. It was approaching closing time and the shop owner was looking nervously at the clock. I was getting hungry and fed up. At that moment, the owner of the shop switched off the pump to the tank. The sound which I had barely noticed before suddenly stopped. The aural landscape, the environment around the boy, had changed. The link had been broken. I saw the boy's shoulders relax. 'Come on, let's go,' I said. And he did.

Which brings us to the question of bribery. In any of the examples given above, a bribe may have worked quicker. A packet of crisps, the promise of the favourite DVD. We've all done it. Sometimes of course it is necessary. In an emergency. You can't mess around with a fire drill for instance. Let alone a real fire. You've just got to get out, and bribery may be the quickest option.

At other times, though, it kind of leaves a bad taste in the mouth. Bribery is giving the wrong message. 'Look, Ben. If you put your coat on I'll give you a packet of crisps.' The problem is, the bribe is rarely linked to the activity itself. It doesn't encourage choice. It doesn't foster a sense of self. Karl may have got out of the car if I had waved a packet of crisps at him from the school gate, but somehow that would have been an insult to him, and to his unique ability to make his own sensible choice to get out when he is ready. It wouldn't have acknowledged the complexity of his feelings that day.

Extreme behaviours

What about the other end of the spectrum of challenging behaviours? The extreme end.

Here's a list, but like all lists in this book, anyone with any experience of working with young people with complex needs will be able to add many more:

> spitting, urinating on the floor, pinching, poking, screaming, crushing, scratching, kicking, defecating on the floor, smashing windows, throwing furniture, undressing in public, eating own continence pad, hitting own head against the wall, smashing crockery, turning over tables, making self sick, handing out nasal mucus, throwing expensive equipment out of window, running into the road, biting self, biting others, pulling things off shelves…

All of these behaviours are certainly egocentric. They are also pre-intentional inasmuch as they are not necessarily intended to affect those around them.

This doesn't mean they are unconscious, that the young person is not aware of what he is doing. We are all aware of what we are doing, whether we have complex needs or not, but we are not necessarily always aware of its impact, consequences or moral repercussions. A young person with complex needs probably even less so. Yes, Ramzi, Ben, most of the others are all capable of consciously bending the rules to suit themselves, but that's just because they are human.

For most of us, our behaviours and responses become tailored to the moral and social expectations of the world we live in. If I get frustrated or angry, I may go quiet or raise my voice, but thankfully I am unlikely to do any of the very challenging behaviours listed above.

People with complex needs get angry and frustrated just like all of us. They undoubtedly suffer from stress and anxiety and will of course also suffer from low moods and depression just like anyone. However, we cannot expect their behaviours to conform to the same moral and social codes.

So again, acceptance is at the heart of the process. Accepting that sometimes, under conditions of extreme duress, some young people with complex needs will literally have no options left but to throw, spit and bite.

Once this stage has been reached, though, there are very few short-term solutions. Realistically, the only option is to try to ensure that the young person is able to work through his anxiety with minimum risk to himself and to others. We have to trust that really extreme behaviour has a shelf life. Sooner or later the storm will pass, stress levels will lower and exhaustion will set in. All we can do is try to make sure everyone, including the person who is upset, is as safe as they possibly can be.

Daniel's most difficult moments usually follow more or less this pattern. His behaviour when he is really upset is very challenging indeed. He will smash windows with his head, bang his forehead so hard against a wall that it bleeds, throw furniture across the room, bite chunks out of his own arms, claw at his own flesh, tear his clothes. Often he will wet or soil himself. His teachers and family have all been injured at times like these. Bitten or scratched. It's not nice at all, but it has its limits. Five, ten minutes of this and Daniel sinks to the floor. Sobbing uncontrollably. He cries and cries till all his energy is spent.

We have watched him of course throughout this. Done all we can to ensure he is safe. Ushered the other students out of the room. When it's over, we make him a cup of tea. We sit with him. Quietly. The episode is over.

There are things we can do, though, to try to ensure that extreme behaviour like Daniel's doesn't happen. Or at least is exceptionally rare. Not short-term solutions. Long-term strategies which start way before the challenging behaviour begins. Usually, only a long-term approach really works.

First, it's important to remember that challenging behaviour rarely occurs in a vacuum, rarely comes absolutely out of nowhere. Right at the beginning of this chapter we said that behaviour is the way we respond to our environment through language and action. Challenging behaviour tends to happen when there is a tension between the person and the environment around him. This is certainly the case when that person has complex needs.

Sometimes that tension can and should be identified early on, especially if it is habitual. Ben, for example, doesn't particularly like sitting in his chair. If he's in it too long, his subsequent behaviour will deteriorate. It's why keeping Ben strapped in his chair just to control him can actually have the opposite effect. Ramzi doesn't like wearing long sleeves. If we make him put on a coat, he may throw himself about, or bite himself. Karl dislikes the noises made by Alice. If they are left together too long, he can get very aggressive.

We may never know what the actual trigger to Daniel's destructive behaviour was, but for him to reach the extreme levels of distress described above, we have already failed him. In the long run up to this destructive behaviour, we have failed to spot the signs. Maybe we have not done enough. Maybe we have done too much. Maybe we have stood too close. Maybe we have used the wrong words. Maybe we have talked too much, or not at all. Maybe we have intervened too soon. Somewhere along the line there may have been a breakdown in communication. And Daniel isn't able to say: 'I'm feeling stressed. Leave me alone. I think I'll just go for a walk.' So the original tension, the original cause of the distress was able to escalate beyond all control or hope of recovery into a spiral of anxiety.

It's why we have to create environments for young people like Daniel which give them the space and time to unwind. To feel themselves again. Environments which suit them and which as far as possible are non-stressful. Colour, the quality of light, the effect of music, space, clarity and calm. The attitudes of the people around them. They are all so important. We will look more closely at these in Chapter 5.

The staff around young people prone to challenging behaviour must be aware of the impact their own behaviour, and especially any anxiety they are carrying with them, can have on their students. It's one of the key qualities required by anyone working in this kind of environment. The ability to lower our own level of arousal to stress, to breathe, to stay still, to slow down, to be calm and focused. Above all to keep it simple. When dealing with a young person like Daniel, less is usually better than more.

Schools which are most effective at dealing with very challenging behaviours have managed to create a whole culture of de-escalation. They have recognised that a long-term strategy of training, support and discussion for the staff is the best way of minimising dangerous incidents. They will have put in place individual behaviour management plans which outline appropriate and long-term strategies to minimise the risk of behaviour getting out of hand.

Often, it is the little things which work best in the long run. The things we can all do very easily. Things we can do all the time, not just when the situation is getting out of control:

- *Proximity.* Many of these young people have been closely monitored, followed and tracked for most of their lives. In a safe, school environment we don't always have to do this. We don't have to sit or stand too close to them. We can give them space. Just be with them, but not too close. We all have a line of personal space behind which we feel secure. So do they.

- *Pace.* It's not only the pace of the lesson itself which might need to be slow to allow students to react and respond.

The staff themselves need to try to keep quick or unexpected movements to a minimum. They should move around the room in a calm and measured way. If the environment around the child is a safe one and if the school is secure it should only very rarely be necessary to run after a young person.

- *Levels.* Nor do we always have to stand over our students. If they are sitting, we can sit too. If they are lying down, so could we. If they are standing or beginning to pace up and down, we don't have to follow them. Sometimes just sitting down quietly ourselves is the best approach. When we sit down, they might learn to sit down.

- *Non-intervention.* Often it's best to just leave well alone. In a safe and supported way. We can be too involved. Left to its own devices, the mind will usually become calm. Often, just letting a young person be for a while will stop the spiral of anxiety getting out of control.

- *Body language.* We should be aware of the messages our own stance and gestures may be giving out. Drop your shoulders. Move more slowly. Consciously relax your arms and legs. Breathe. Smile. It may just be what Daniel needs to see and feel today.

- *Voice and speech.* Give clear, simple, quiet instructions. Don't ask too much at a time. Keep your voice as calm as possible. Try to be aware when your own stress is coming out in your speech.

- *The 'no' line.* Where do we draw the 'no' line? Perhaps we have drawn it too close? Perhaps we are saying 'no' just too soon or too often? Try not to overdo the negative. Leave 'no' until the very last moment, until it counts, until we really mean it. Why am I saying 'no' at this moment anyway? Is it really necessary at this point?

Spitting

Some behaviours don't have an obvious build-up. They may be harder to see coming, are less physically destructive or violent but no less challenging. Of these, spitting is often the one which is hardest to cope with. Ramzi, for example, may be sitting apparently normally in a chair. There are no obvious signs he is getting upset. So you ask him to take part in an activity. He spits in your face.

Spitting is culturally and socially taboo for all sorts of reasons, and rightly so. It's about as offensive as you can get. For Ramzi though, and for many others, it may be an extension of his oral/ projectile approach to the world. Ramzi throws things, and puts things in his mouth. A spit is just a synthesis of the two. A means of communication which often gets a communication in return.

How do we respond? Do we tell him off? It's hard not to. But what does 'telling off' mean to Ramzi? To any young person with complex needs?

If I tell a boy off in a mainstream setting, there is a good chance he will understand that he has breached some rule or behavioural code. He may modify his behaviour as a result. Ramzi may recognise the changed tone in my voice, he may understand on one level that I am angry, but does he fully understand the complex moral and cultural background to a spit? I suspect not. We may just have to accept that for Ramzi my raised voice and confrontational stance, my wagging finger, are in fact communications which on one level he may enjoy. Why not? It's human communication after all.

All advice and experience suggests that ignoring spitting is the only effective response. It's a long-term solution to this particular problem which seems to work more than others. As a teacher, I am prepared to do it, even if it means getting spit in my hair and in my clothes. Sooner or later Ramzi will move on. He will seek other communicative channels.

Of course, on this particular issue, I don't think we can expect everyone to react in the same way. With spitting at least, and maybe one or two other unpleasant behaviours, a consistent approach is rarely possible. If one of the team is having a bad day, and when

Ramzi spits at her she shouts at him, well, Ramzi may be learning that the world isn't so predictable after all.

Sexualised behaviours

Finally, a brief word about sexualised behaviours. I say brief because every school, every state, every country will have its own policies and protocols with regard to this subject. Also, people working in this environment are likely to have a wide range of cultural, moral or religious attitudes.

What I will say is this. This book is primarily about young people with complex needs aged between 14 and 19. Young people in this age bracket experience emerging sexual feelings as strongly as anybody else of their age. What they don't and may never understand are the social rules, taboos and legal frameworks which prohibit open displays of their sexuality.

Self-stimulation in class or in other public places will be quite common, as will the exposure of intimate parts of the body. Exploring their own and their classmates' bodies in what could be said to be sexualised ways may also happen.

Whatever the response agreed by the school or governing body, it should be consistent and be based on an acceptance of the young person's needs, respect for his or her dignity and privacy, and a commitment to ensuring young people are not ever being put into a position where they are likely to be vulnerable to abuse.

In the next chapter we are going to attempt to answer the question: *'What do you actually teach them?'*

Chapter 4

'What Do You Actually Teach Them?'

In teaching young people with the most complex needs, it's very easy for our practice to be restricted by narrow definitions of common terms. Terms such as 'curriculum', 'learning' and 'teaching' for instance. Even the word 'lesson'. It can be hard for us to think about how to personalise learning if we stick rigidly to the more generally accepted definitions of these terms.

The word 'curriculum' tends in mainstream practice to mean a set of objective facts which make up a 'subject' or part of a 'subject'. 'Learning' tends to refer to the acquisition of knowledge or skills. 'Teaching' tends to mean the transmission of the facts or of a whole curriculum so that 'learning' takes place; and a 'lesson' tends to be a period of time devoted to that process.

These definitions are false friends when it comes to teaching young people with complex and unique needs.

I would love to set out one day to 'teach' Daniel a few words of French, a couple of phrases maybe. That would be my 'curriculum'. Not his, but mine. I'd teach him how to say the words, and what they mean in a lesson lasting 50 minutes. He'd 'learn' the words and phrases, possibly by rote, and the following week I might even test him on them. It would all be very neat and tidy and I'd feel very pleased with myself.

I need to be completely realistic, though. In fact, being completely realistic is my only option when working with Daniel, or Alice, or Sammy or any of the others.

Although Daniel is able to articulate a few recognisable English words, he is likely to become even more anxious than usual if I start speaking to him in French. I suspect he has no real concept of 'otherness', as in other languages, or other countries. He may become so anxious that he attacks or bites me. These behavioural issues mean that it is unlikely that his parents would ever consider taking him on holiday to France.

I am struggling here to find any reason to teach Daniel French at all. Tasting a newly baked baguette of course, or smelling the wonderful aromas from some French cooking: those I can justify as part of an experiential sensory curriculum. But actually teaching Daniel French: I can't really make a case for it.

I would probably reach the same conclusion with many of the more traditional curriculum subjects. They are just not right for Daniel.

The reason the question *'What do you actually teach them?'* cannot be answered with a simple sentence is that certain words have to be redefined.

What is a curriculum?

A curriculum for any young person with complex learning difficulties, especially those in the 14–19 age range, must be a direct response to his or her actual needs. It has to grow out of everything we know about them. So, if there are 12 students in a class, there will be 12 curricula.

Alice's curriculum, for example, must be based on Alice: her own needs, wants and abilities. It must come out of what we know about her, and what her parents, carers and other specialists know about her and want for her. We have to provide something relevant to her age as well. At school she will be amongst students with more moderate learning difficulties who have a more mature timetable. Alice has the right to a mature, age-appropriate curriculum too.

It should be a curriculum which equips her to be safe and secure within herself and within her environment, to lead as fulfilling and as happy a life as possible, to be cared for and supported, but not to be passive or helpless. A curriculum which is holistic, meaning that it will address Alice as a whole person, and include not only her immediate learning needs, but also her need for personal care, physiotherapy, massage, alternative therapies, her own space, etc. A curriculum drawn up not by one teacher, but by everyone involved with her. A curriculum which doesn't just start and end at the school gates.

It should be a curriculum which provides Alice with a sense of autonomy. A curriculum which takes as a starting point where Alice is now, and prepares her for her future life. To a large degree, a curriculum that Alice initiates herself, by what she does, and tries to do.

So what do we call a curriculum like this? I think 'personalised' is the only option.

What is learning?

With such a diverse and layered curriculum, we need to be as bold as possible in our definition of 'learning'. We must be prepared to embrace learning in all its forms if we are to personalise it for each of our students.

Learning through experience

Process-based learning. Learning by doing.

Spending time with someone new. That is learning. Walking with just one other person to the shop and carrying your own small bag of shopping back with you. That is learning. Getting on a bus and going to town for the first time. That is learning. Sitting quietly in a circle just listening to some music. That is learning. And as Edward's dad asks for in the interview in Chapter 8: a few white-knuckle rides. Maybe not so much learning, but certainly wonderful experiences.

Learning new life skills

Sammy may be learning to use a fork, hand over hand at first, then more independently. Daniel may be learning how to make a sandwich for himself. A long process, but Daniel is the kind of boy who may well achieve this. Kyle has a real interest in the SMART board. He may need to learn how to change from one software application to another.

Life skills linked to personal care can also be taught, modelled and practised: combing hair, cleaning teeth, washing hands all encourage autonomy. Our students may never master these skills totally, but being involved in the process, even with close support, can be empowering.

Learning what it feels like not to be restricted

For a young ambulant person with complex needs just to wander round the school being only shadowed by a carer may feel very new and liberating.

Learning what it's like to be in charge for once

In charge of deciding who will get the beanbag next. In charge of giving out the percussion instruments. In charge of the class register. In tiny but significant ways to be in charge of your own world.

Learning when apparently not learning

All those moments which take students away from class: personal care, moving from one part of the school to another, seeing the occupational therapist, massage, having lunch. All these are opportunities for learning. Learning about change, learning about movement, learning about working with and communicating with other people, feeling more comfortable with your own body.

Tangential learning

As teachers we know that learning is more than just a journey from A to B. In going from A to B, we often learn C. Nowhere is that more true than with a PMLD class.

Sammy is in an ICT lesson. I want him to be able to use some touch screen technology. That is what I want him to learn today. On my lesson plan, that might be his target. By the end of the lesson he may have achieved it. If he has, I'll be pleased. I'll certainly give him lots of praise and encouragement. I might even given him a sticker, or a certificate. He may be able to do it again the next day, or the week after. He may do it correctly for the rest of his life. He may not. That's only one issue. Because while learning, or not, that task, Sammy may have had the chance to be involved in at least the following other opportunities for learning:

- being with a group
- sitting next to a new person
- being in a different room
- saying hello
- closing the blinds
- switching on and off the lights when asked
- communicating with others.

In fact, Sammy's greatest achievement in this lesson might well have been sitting for 20 minutes in the same place without putting his hands inside the shirt of the person next to him. That may be more worthy of praise and reward for Sammy than the simple fact that he used a bit of software correctly. He may understand his teacher's genuine and heartfelt praise for behaving appropriately more acutely than he understands the response to achieving his target for the lesson.

Learning to make connections

Games and activities which match colours, shapes, qualities of texture and sound, letters and words even. Object permanence and linking things that are and then aren't there. These are first steps towards making wider connections, towards seeing a bigger picture, towards understanding oneself and others.

Learning transferable skills

Skills gained through subjects such as numeracy, ICT, art, food technology, or through activities, games and puzzles which may have wider implications for a student's life.

Ramzi can nearly do his own Velcro shoes up. The fine motor skills developed doing shape puzzles or abacus games in a numeracy class, or anywhere really, may help him with this in the future.

Jane Barbrook is a numeracy specialist who has many years' experience teaching young people with complex needs. I asked her what sort of skills a student can gain in a numeracy class. She places particular emphasis on problem solving:

> For older learners with profound and multiple learning difficulties, 'mathematics' is primarily about developing their skills to solve practical and meaningful problems in a range of contexts. Problem solving – using real objects in real-life situations so that the young adult can discover relationships with position (themselves, other people, objects and materials); to develop their sensory awareness; and to learn about quantities (one, lots, more) through supported exploration. As these skills develop the young person learns to make choices and decisions in real-life contexts.
>
> Problem solving can be reinforced when working on individual targets throughout daily routines and importantly through sensory, social and 'play' activities when the learners are interacting with their environment and with other people.

Problem solving is in itself a key type of learning in any personalised curriculum.

In a safe and supported way, Usha needs to be allowed to work out her own way of getting from A to B in the classroom. Kyle tends to try to hold his school diary in one hand and his bag in another when he leaves school. This means he has no hands left to pull himself up into his bus. For Kyle, the 'problem' to be solved is how to get his book into his bag so that he has one hand free. We could do it for him of course, but for Kyle, it will be a real-life skill and should be part of his curriculum.

If a curriculum is truly personalised on each individual student, then everything he or she does in numeracy, or arts and crafts, or music, or food technology or ICT will have a direct and real relevance. All learnt skills will potentially be transferable to other aspects of a young person's life in and out of school. The subject itself in many ways is secondary to the real curriculum: the personal curriculum. Subjects are frameworks, they give a structure, create a theme, or provide a student with a transferable skill for his whole life.

Lucie Calow has over 20 years' experience in special education and is currently Headteacher of Granta School in Cambridgeshire in the UK. She believes passionately that skills acquired by a young person with complex needs in the classroom must be of use to them beyond school:

> It is possible to teach a student to undertake a task or to be able to communicate in a particular session, but this needs to be a useful tool across settings if it is going to have maximum impact. There is nothing wrong with saying, for example, that a student can complete a particular puzzle in class using 12 pieces and that he gains satisfaction and enjoyment in doing that. However, to be able to complete similar 12 piece puzzles at home, at respite, at school, gives him a satisfying hobby for life.

Arts and crafts, cookery, design and technology all provide fantastic opportunities for our students to engage, to try out, to initiate, to respond, to develop.

We have to allow the students to be truly involved at all levels, though. Feeling, tasting, smelling, pouring, mixing, squashing, rubbing, stirring, crushing, tasting some more, watching flour fall through light, splattering paint, squishing clay, breaking eggs, throwing cherries. A cake may be inedible, a painting or a sculpture indecipherable. That's not the point. The students will have initiated, taken part, been involved, and what a wonderful, sensory experiential learning experience they will have had.

Personal issues like the developing body, feelings, religious and cultural beliefs and practices may well not be understood in any concrete way by a student with complex needs, but can still be acknowledged and celebrated through sign and symbol, colour and sound.

Capturing the moment, building on engagement, managing behaviour, fostering autonomy, giving responsibility, developing communication: all have as much relevance in a cookery class as they do in a communications class.

Community trips as well are a wonderful learning experience. Some of our students can do real-life things like choosing drinks and handing over money. Meetings between young people with complex needs and members of the public are awareness-raising exercises for everyone.

Potentially then, everything, each moment, is 'learning', or at the very least 'experience', and as long as it is backed up with enough positive support and encouragement, and then followed up, maybe repeated several times over the following weeks, experience may become 'learning' too.

There is one important rule, though. Not unique to PMLD groups, but more significant here than any other form of teaching and learning. Students who are anxious or under stress will not learn effectively, and in the case of a student with complex needs, will probably not learn at all. In Chapter 5 we'll be looking at how to create environments for learning which are as stress-free as possible.

What is teaching?

Kyle is ready and willing to learn how to prepare his own drinks. We would be failing him if we didn't take this on. It will involve many of the traditional skills of any good teacher: demonstration, modelling, verbal and physical prompting. Hand over hand guidance. It will take a lot of repetition, plenty of spilt drinks, but it will be worth it in the end. We will have taught Kyle how to do something useful to him.

In fact the traditional skills and techniques of any good teacher are no less important in a complex needs setting as anywhere else: setting the right pace for a lesson, stop/go and burst/pause activities; waiting for the student to respond; putting each student first; giving positive feedback; careful planning.

For all the ways Kyle, and Daniel, and Alice and the others learn, their teachers will have to be able to adopt at least as many methods. The teaching has to be just as broad and eclectic as the learning, and above all student-centred.

Often the phrase 'student-centred' is just a nice expression used in a prospectus. But in a special school we have no choice, and that is one of the joys of this kind of work. Student-centred teaching is what we do. Working in a special school is exciting because it reminds us why we teach.

Teaching will be cooperative as well: working next to and with the students, with colleagues and with a host of other professionals. A multi-agency approach.

Teaching will be inclusive: trying to include all the students as individually as possible in the learning process. It will involve standing in front of a student, sitting on a chair next to a student, lying on the floor with a student, 'talking' with a student who can only make guttural noises. Just being with a student. Quietly and non-judgementally.

Teaching may involve role-play: practising for real-life situations like finding your coat, or handing over money in a shop. It'll definitely be interactive, usually experiential, and occasionally transformational.

Sometimes teachers of young people with complex needs will be observers, often facilitators, and frequently protectors. They will know when to intervene, but they will also know when to step back. Step back, but not switch off. That's the key I think. Stepping back and allowing Alice to hold that brush loaded with red paint. Waiting and watching to see what she does. Encouraging her gently to place it on the large white paper in front of her. It may end up on the floor. It may end up in Alice's mouth. It may end up on the paper. That's not the point. The teacher will have learnt something valuable about Alice. Alice may have learnt something about colour, weight and balance. Maybe something that can be built on in the future.

Teachers will be communication partners, watching and waiting for their students to respond or engage. Looking for moments of connection. They will know how to catch a moment – the moment Ramzi gets up and engages in something for instance – and build on it.

They will be exhausted, because they will never be able to switch off – always aware of what is going on everywhere in the room. Above all, though, they will be patient.

They will be prepared to take risks. Often they will succeed. Sometimes, spectacularly, they won't...

Once, I was waiting on The Strand in London's West End for a coach to come and pick us all up after a theatre trip. I was supporting a boy of about 17 with complex needs. Let's call him Jake. I was holding Jake's hand of course, but at the same time I was congratulating myself on the fact that Jake had come to London, sat through a whole musical, and was now experiencing the hustle and bustle of a London rush hour with all its noise and colour and people. What a wonderful sensory experience for Jake!

I noticed that people walking past were looking at Jake with a little too much attention. Smiling. Frowning. I looked at him. His trousers and underwear were round his ankles. He was naked from the waist down.

What is a lesson?

A lesson can be any time, anywhere, any place. In a personalised environment, a lesson takes place at the moment where a student engages and is ready to learn. It takes place at the moment of communication, which can be at any moment, in any place and in any way.

Traditional lesson structures such as the three-part lesson are fine. Our students need to experience a beginning, middle and an end to things as well. That's kind of the structure of most things in life too.

It is important too that our students experience working in large and small groups, in pairs, and one-to-one. Sitting at tables, sitting on soft chairs. Sitting with someone. Sitting on their own. These are all social norms they will experience again and again in their lives, and which they will need to be ready for.

Planning a lesson is vital too. Teaching a PMLD class has to be both carefully prepared for and allowed to take its own course. The teacher has to prepare the room, the resources, the staff and the activities. Usually, in a personalised environment there will be as many activities as there are students, or realistically, the same number of activities as there are staff available to lead them.

A lesson should not be so rigorously prepared, though, that it cannot be changed or adapted according to circumstance. Often, learning, or an opportunity for learning, may happen unexpectedly, and staff must be ready to spot that engagement and build on it. If Sammy takes the book his teacher is reading with him and drops it on the floor, then gets up, goes to the bookshelf and finds a different book, perhaps that should be the book for Sammy today. He has made a perfectly valid communication for an 18-year-old and deserves to have it acknowledged.

If a lesson is planned in such a way that a personal care or medical issue comes as a surprise or an inconvenience, then perhaps the structure of that lesson does not really favour personalisation. Personal care is as much a part of a curriculum as anything else.

Sports, walks, massage, sensory sessions, class meetings, relaxation, lunch. All these are lessons too, because all are opportunities for learning.

So that's the answer to the question, really. '*What do you actually teach them?*' We teach them what they need and we teach it to them in a way that suits them.

Above all, we teach them to be happy, to communicate a little better and to be as independent as possible. The Big Three that their parents and carers usually want.

Being happy

If I were teaching maths to a class of mainstream students, I would want them to enjoy my class. I know they will learn better if they are happy. But I also want them to be able to do the maths. This will take hard work. So in trying to get them to a certain level in maths, my commitment to their happiness might slip a little and be replaced by a desire for them to learn and achieve. As an exam approaches I might find myself not caring very much at all about their happiness.

In a PMLD classroom, it's kind of the other way round. The happiness, the well-being of the students, should be right up there, all the time. Because when Ramzi, or Sammy, or Usha laugh – which they do quite a lot – their laughter, their happiness is just as valid, just as all-embracing, just as real as anybody else's. Like all of us, it probably means they are happy; it usually means they are comfortable. It might just mean they are at ease with themselves. Which when you have spent your whole life being observed, followed, toileted, strapped into cars and chairs, lifted, fed and told 'no', is a pretty precious thing.

Can happiness be taught? Probably not, but it can be modelled and encouraged. External circumstances can be arranged to make it likely. A student is far more likely to feel comfortable and happy if their personal care is dealt with professionally and sensitively, for instance. We can also create environments using space, colour and sound which prioritise the comfort, calmness and well-being of our students. We'll be looking at this in Chapter 5.

We can make happiness more likely by making sure that praise and positive reinforcement are at the heart of what we do. We must thank, smile, chat, laugh and share. It will all contribute to making the students feel they are in a good place.

Friendship is part of well-being too. A friend is someone who accepts us as we are. Through thick and thin. So for the students, many of their teachers and carers will and should be their friends.

Precisely because there has been such a close link between students with complex needs and their teachers or carers, they may not have spent much time with others of more or less their own age to form friendships. Nor have they tended to be left to their own devices in playgrounds or at parties to experiment with social relationships. But that doesn't mean they don't want or need friendships. No matter how old they are, it's never too late to allow them to explore social relationships. That's how we all learn.

It can seem risky, though, to allow, say, Daniel and Ramzi to spend time together in a relatively unstructured way, just 'hanging out'. Quite naturally we don't want either of them to come to any harm. We might be unsure how they might react to each other if left to their own devices. We do need to take the risk, though, of allowing them to just be with each other. They will need to be watched of course, but like all of us they will learn from spending time with people they like. It's liberating for us too to realise that they are able, even for relatively short periods of time, to occupy themselves socially.

Ben really enjoys spending time with another student, Alfie, outside on the grass playing with his wheelchair. They both like pushing it up and down. Ben also likes Alfie to sit in it so he can push him. Alfie will maybe do this once or twice, but soon gets fed up with it. He shows that he has had enough by turning his back on Ben, or sitting down on the grass. Ben can get quite insistent of course and start pulling Alfie by the shirt, or grabbing his arm. This is the point where a member of staff will usually intervene and explain to Ben that Alfie has had enough.

Edward really likes Ramzi, and enjoys spending time with him. He also likes pushing Ramzi gently. Sometimes, this makes them both laugh, and they might do this for ten minutes or more. Ramzi usually tires of this first and gently pushes Edward away. Sometimes Edward doesn't get the message and carries on. Ramzi can get a bit cross and pushes Edward harder. Edward then usually understands that Ramzi has had enough or a member of staff gently separates them and explains to Edward that Ramzi has had enough for today.

In all sorts of ways, this is the structure of all nascent friendships the world over. We've all learnt through the joys and knock-backs of making and losing friends. It seems a shame to stop it happening just because someone is labelled as having 'complex needs'.

Communication

To create a personalised curriculum around communication, we must first refer to advice from other agencies around the young person, and especially speech and language therapists. Each student should have a personalised speech and language plan outlining their abilities and needs, with targets for development.

In drawing up these plans, we must look in the long term. We and the other specialists involved have to be realistic about each young person's current abilities and future needs, and realistic about equipping them with communication skills which will be of use to them in the future.

We must have as broad and eclectic a view as possible of what we mean by communication. Depending on the needs and abilities of the child, any number of modes of communication can be valid. Every behaviour, every sound, every gesture, from the smallest movement of an eye to the mad dash across the room, can be seen as communication. Sometimes we will understand it, often we won't. Sometimes it will be appropriate, sometimes it won't. But we must be ready to notice when communication is taking place and, if we can, to respond.

Shelley Lockwood is an Intensive Interaction practitioner and co-ordinator of the Intensive Interaction Regional Support Network in Cambridge, UK (http://www.intensiveinteraction. co.uk/regional-networks/cambridge.html). I interviewed her for this book. Her definition of Intensive Interaction is a good way of summarising the whole approach to personalising the curriculum for young people with complex needs, and in particular to our approach to communication. She talks of '*building meaningful social relationships based on mutual respect and trust by engaging in warm genuine exchanges, conversations or moments of connection whenever or wherever possible.*'

It is precisely these 'moments of connection' that are so important.

Of the students we are getting to know in this book, only Daniel is able to speak a few recognisable words. Conventional language, though, is clearly a concept that is within his grasp. For this reason, the staff around Daniel need to ensure they talk with him in clear short sentences, ask him questions he is able to understand and respond to, and above all, give him the opportunity to use what words and expressions he already has in real or simulated real-life situations. He is a nervous boy, so new words will need to be introduced carefully and slowly. We may need to draw up a list of words and very short phrases which may be of use to him in the coming years and especially when he leaves school. These won't necessarily be the same words we would expect a neuro-typical child to learn in the early years of language acquisition.

Of the others, Ben tries to make words. He can make a 'b' sound very well, and often says 'yeah' or 'no' in more or less appropriate places. As with Daniel, it will be important to encourage and build on this, especially as he thrives on human contact and may enjoy copying and echoing games with an attentive adult. It is possible that over time he may in this way learn a wider repertoire of sounds and possibly some new words.

Ramzi and Kyle make sounds which are made up of vowels and consonants. Their language is quite complex and clearly has meaning for them. It deserves to be recognised and affirmed for what it is, and the staff around them need to be prepared to use it with them.

Communicative sounds, no matter what they are like, deserve to be listened to, echoed or copied. Only in this way will Ramzi, Kyle and other young people with similar language profiles have the chance of understanding that they are able to communicate, and that somebody will listen and respond. They may never use conventional language, but they will be involved in a meaningful process of shared communication. It will be good for them, and in the long run it may lead to the acquisition of further sounds.

Sammy used to speak a little when he was much younger, but now is almost completely silent. However, he does appear to enjoy 'mouthing' words. Again, as with Ramzi and Kyle, it is important for the staff around Sammy to value this as a form of language by mirroring or copying his mouth movements, maybe accompanying them with sounds at times. Sammy may never speak again, but he has the right to have his own unique attempts valued and encouraged.

It's what Shelley Lockwood calls being a *valued fellow-member of a social group or community*. It's what we all want and need, whether we have complex needs or not.

For all the young people though, whether they are in any way verbal or not, being involved in 'chat' is very important. Staff should be prepared to chat with them in clear, simple terms. Talk about the weather, share the latest school news. The young person may not understand the content of what is being said, but they will be involved in a mature socio-dynamic relationship with someone who values them as a communication partner.

Communication takes place on so much more than just the verbal level, of course. Reaching out, waving arms, kicking legs, moving the head, pointing with the eyes, touching: these are all forms of communication.

Usha's friend Mary is almost permanently in a chair and has no language, but she loves someone just touching the palms of her hands. She responds with smiles and sounds of joy. It's a very important means of communication for Mary.

Sometimes, the simple act of massaging someone's hands can lead to a meaningful communication. Sammy, say, or Mary, have no recognisable verbal communication. Mary has very little movement. But they both love physical contact. They particularly love having their hands gently massaged. This needn't be a passive thing, though, where they just 'receive' a massage. If we pause after each gentle massage, Mary may well initiate the next massage, perhaps by just a tiny movement of her hand or a small vocalisation. Sammy may reach out and pull your hand towards his. They are communicating in clear, valid and understandable ways. Their own ways.

There are of course a variety of systems of augmentative or alternative communication (AAC) available which can replace speech, and allow people who are non-verbal to express preferences, choices, needs and feelings in other concrete forms. Systems such as objects of reference, environmental cues, symbols, picture exchange systems, signing, and switch-based speech output devices such as Bigmack, Go Talk, Nova Chat and eye-operated assistive technologies.

A speech and language therapist will decide in association with the teacher and other specialists which of these methods suits the young person best, and how and when they should be introduced. Again, the approach should be broad and eclectic, introducing each one slowly and never being afraid to abandon one and adopt another, or try a combination if it seems to suit a particular student.

A lot of young non-verbal people with complex needs can and will learn to say, for example, 'I want a drink' by either using an object such as a cup or straw, signing, holding up a symbol or a photo of the desired object, or pressing a switch which activates a pre-recorded voice. They may also be able to respond to questions about their feelings by signing or using photos and symbols which represent 'sad', 'happy' or 'angry' for instance.

The important thing, though, in teaching any of these communication systems is that they can only be taught, and learnt, when there is a real purpose behind the need to communicate.

For example, there is little point trying to teach Kyle to use a picture symbol to ask for a drink at a time when he doesn't normally have a drink or has shown no interest in having one. The impetus, the drive for getting a drink must come from him first. Only then can an object symbol or sign be introduced with purpose and meaning.

Similarly, in a classroom environment, it may be perfectly acceptable for Sammy to get up and go to the toilet without using a symbol or sign. Out in the community in an unfamiliar place though, he may need to 'ask'. So even though he is 18 and can manage the toilet independently, it may be appropriate to give him the toilet symbol or picture, or at least show it to him whenever he uses the toilet in class. Then, when he is in the community, he can take the symbol with him and use it when he needs to.

We must also be absolutely realistic about whether the young person understands in a constructive way the use of a particular method before including it as part of their communication package. We must be prepared to ask difficult questions. For example, does a photo of the local supermarket actually represent the supermarket for Alice? If she does see the picture as the object it represents, does it mean 'We are going to the supermarket?' or does it just mean 'supermarket'? Maybe it just means 'picture'?

These are questions which it is always going to be difficult to answer and can only be tested by trial and error, repetition and constant fulfilment of the objective. In other words, if being exposed to the picture of the supermarket is very closely followed by actually going to the supermarket, and by reinforcing the photo when she is at the supermarket itself, it is more likely than not that over time Alice will begin to associate the photo with a trip to the supermarket. Even then, it is an inexact science.

Sometimes, it may be difficult for a student to learn a particular method because he may have other uses for the resources required. Alfie for instance may well find signing easier than using a symbol-base system because he can't help putting the paper symbols in his mouth. Kyle might be easily distracted by the play of light on laminated card, while Edward may never use symbols effectively because he prefers flicking them across the room.

An alternative or augmentative system must always be used for a reason, and not just because it is there.

Kyle, for example, takes me by the hand, leads me to the kitchen unit and puts my hand on a bottle of squash. That is just as valid and useful a means of communicating as any other, and what is more, it doesn't require any expensive or carefully prepared resources. It is initiated totally by Kyle himself. It's a skill he can take easily into whatever educational or care environment he finds himself in for the rest of his life.

This is another important point. Particularly for older students, we must always bear in mind whether a system will be useful and accessible to the student beyond the relatively controlled conditions of a classroom. Is it a resource that they are likely to have access to or even afford out in the community, at home or in a respite setting? By the time they leave school, any alternative system used by a student must be personalised to him or her. They must be able to use it at their own initiative if appropriate and it should be accessible, understandable and affordable to future carers or other professionals.

But communication isn't always about making clear and direct requests for something, or expressing choices. It can be as simple as passing a ball around a group, or throwing a beanbag back and forth. Giving and taking. Throwing and catching. They are all communicative. What Shelley Lockwood calls *the value and power of making fundamental human, social connections with other people*.

On a very important level, communication is often simply about being with someone, perhaps silently, perhaps just with a few words or a gentle touch. Perhaps just reading quietly with them. To quote Shelley Lockwood again:

> *Conversation does not need to employ speech. It can retain more of its original meaning of 'to abide or keep company with', and is an*

expression of social connection which might be communicated simply *by being genuinely present with someone.*

This means being with our students without an intention to interact. Just letting them know they are accepted, non-judgementally, as they are.

So, our curriculum, *what we actually teach them*, is about supporting them to be happy, to communicate as well as they can, and to be as independent as possible. These three can only be learnt in a personalised way. Sammy's communication is not Kyle's. Independence for Usha is not the same as independence for Alice. Daniel's feelings of joy and comfort will only ever be uniquely his own.

The curriculum is the student; the student is the curriculum. Alice's curriculum looks like Alice. Ben's looks like Ben.

Independence

What do we mean by 'independence' or 'autonomy' in the context of a group of students with complex needs? It's important to be able to redefine here, because these are terms which are central to the whole question of personalisation.

Sammy is 'independent' inasmuch as he has his own house, but he shares it with his two full-time carers. He couldn't possibly be left there alone. Ramzi loves spending the day with his dad in the delivery lorry, but it's not Ramzi's job. Independence for Sammy and Ramzi is about smaller, but no less significant things. When Sammy finds his own shoe, instead of a teacher finding it for him: that is independence.

There are real domestic skills we can and should teach some of the students to help them live more independent lives. It's a question of identifying which skills each individual student can potentially embrace. Skills which will be relevant to him or her now and in the future.

For example, there is no physical reason why Daniel shouldn't be able to prepare his own tea in a safe and supported way. He is also a boy who can learn by modelling and observation. It'll be important to analyse the steps he needs to take to make a cup of tea, and to identify the ones which may present danger. Making a cup of tea is a personalised life skill for Daniel based on his unique needs and abilities.

Kyle, on the other hand is a little insecure physically and though he doesn't actually fall over, he often stumbles or drops onto his knees. It's clearly not going to be appropriate or safe at this stage in his life to teach him a skill like making a cup of tea. However, he has shown an interest in where the fruit juice is kept and once he tried to take the lid off the bottle. He also knows where the cups are.

This is one of those opportunities where the risk is minimal. Kyle has already clearly shown intention and engagement, now we need to create the environment and arrange the circumstances to allow him to undertake more and more of the task autonomously. Perhaps we need to make sure there is only ever a small amount of liquid in the squash bottle? This will make it lighter and easier for Kyle to manipulate. Perhaps we need to loosen the lid a bit, and ensure Kyle's cup is always accessible? We may need to support him at first using hand over hand, for a few weeks even, but there will come a moment when we will just have to step back and let him get on with it. There may be a few spillages, a couple of dropped cups, a change of shirt once or twice, but only by giving Kyle the chance to fulfil his intention will he ever be able to become more autonomous in this one small significant way.

These moments of domestic independence don't have to be as big as making a drink. Allowing Usha, even if only for a few seconds, to feel what it's like to hold her own cup, rather than have someone holding it for her, that is independence too.

But independence isn't only about domestic skills. For the student, it's about intentionality and engagement, gaining confidence and having a sense of self. Actually, it's about growing up in the same way we all do: by trying out new things. By moving from being dependent to being slightly more independent. For Kyle or Sammy, walking from the classroom to the field without having someone holding their arm may be just as significant for them, just as scary, as it is for their brothers and sisters to go off to college for the first time.

Aaron is a 17-year-old boy who is in a chair, is dependent on others for all his personal care needs, and can only really move one hand a little. He cannot take anything by mouth and is fed through a tube to his stomach. His vision is poor. If we look at his UK National Curriculum P-Levels, we see that he is around P1(i) and P1(ii). That is to say, he encounters activities and experiences, shows simple reflex responses, and sometimes focuses his attention on certain people or events.

Yet none of this means he can't display independence. A large accessible switch device is linked to coloured lights and placed under his fingers when he is lying on a bed. The lights are strung on a frame above him. At first, nothing happens. Then you notice the lights going on and off. Aaron, often quite restless, is still and calm. His eyes, which usually wander, fix on the lights. With the smallest of movements of two of his fingers he is controlling the lights. He is in charge of his world. That too is independence.

For the teacher, it's about creating a safe environment or a situation where the student is allowed to do things for himself or herself. It's about stepping back. Sometimes, it's only if you take a step back that the young person is able to take a step forward.

So many of these young people will have been 'done to' over the course of their lives. They have been passive receivers of care. In the school environment we are there to encourage them to be as independent as possible in their own way, and we must try to infuse almost every moment in the classroom where it is feasible and safe with an opportunity for them to act independently.

Ben pulls at the door of the locked cupboard where his favourite drum is kept. There is real intentionality in that. If I then open the door myself, pick up the drum and give it to him, I am not fostering Ben's autonomy. It will save time for me, but then, this isn't about me.

I will have to unlock the door of course, but then I will stand back and let Ben engage in the process of getting his drum himself.

It might mean a couple of boxes knocked over in the process, but he will have expressed his intention, and engaged in a mainly autonomous way in getting it out. For Ben, that is as important an expression of independence as any other 17-year-old's life choices.

I want to take Usha out on the field. But she's holding one of her shoes. The easy thing for me to do would be quickly to take Usha's shoe from her and put it on her. But where is Usha's autonomy in that? Maybe Usha doesn't want her shoe on? If the weather is warm, why shouldn't she be in bare feet? Plenty of 16-year-old girls are like that. But if for some reason it's important for her to have her shoes on, she still needs to be involved in as autonomous a way as possible. Maybe I will take the time to ask Usha to give me her shoe, and explain why, which may involve repeating myself several times. It may take ten minutes, but if she finally gives me her shoe, she has acted autonomously, and been involved in the process of preparing to go outside.

A bit like managing behaviour, it might mean re-appraising a little what is important in the school or classroom environment. Of course there are deadlines to follow, timetables to be kept, and fitting in with those is also part of learning for a young person with complex needs. But sometimes we have to be prepared to be flexible and patient in order to allow our students the time to communicate and respond on their terms.

We have to be prepared to ask ourselves what is more important: that Alice is on time for her ICT class or that she opens the door herself? That a lesson ends exactly on time, or that Ramzi is allowed to fulfil his last-minute decision to work at the SMART board? That personal care is a rushed and undignified event, or is a gentle and careful process which makes the young person feel valued?

We have to value our students' efforts in class no matter how chaotic or messy. It's not about the end product: a perfectly baked cake for instance, or an exactly symmetrical star for the top of the Christmas tree. It's about providing opportunities for each student to engage as autonomously as possible in a task.

Ben is walking round the school one day. Not being 'led' but being allowed to lead. More or less where he wants. He isn't alone, though, he is being shadowed by a member of staff. An 'attentive adult'. Just behind him. So that if he tries to open the door of a classroom or grab someone he passes in the corridor, his 'shadow' can gently guide him away.

He goes to the school hall and finds a large tricycle. Adult size. He pretty soon works out that it moves in a certain way, so he pulls and pushes it backwards and forwards. The member of staff gets on it and cycles it round the hall. Ben thinks this is fantastic. He laughs and claps.

The next day, Ben doesn't seem to want to stay in the class. He seems keen to leave and walk round the school. It's not exactly on the timetable but the teacher lets him go, shadowed again by an attentive adult. He finds himself in the hall again. He finds the trike. After a short while pushing and pulling it, he begins banging the saddle and making high-pitched noises. The member of staff gets on the trike and rides it round. Ben laughs and claps.

This happens a couple of times a week for about a month. Then one day, Ben tries to get on the trike himself. Because his feet are slightly malformed he needs help, but eventually he manages it and is strapped in by the adult.

And so it goes on, small incremental steps, each one initiated by Ben himself. So that now, three months later, Ben asks for 'trike time' using a large photo of himself on the trike, or by turning his hands round like a wheel, or sometimes by trying to say 'bike', which for him is a better word than 'trike' because he can make a 'B' sound but not a 'T' sound. He rides round the school grounds with an adult simply holding the back of the trike lightly when necessary.

He even insists on wearing the safety belt.

Feeling independent. Doing things for ourselves. It's what we all value. It makes us feel whole. It's good for us. It's how we learn. It's no different for young people with profound and multiple learning difficulties no matter how dependent they appear to be on others.

There's one thing, though, which I think is absolutely essential to any curriculum, which we will look at next.

Fresh air and physical exercise

Many of our young people with complex needs have for one reason or another probably spent more time indoors than their mainstream peers. More time inactive too. Not only for their own safety, but also because indoors they are perhaps easier to manage. Some may have spent more time strapped into a wheelchair than is strictly necessary.

For perfectly understandable reasons, their parents and carers have been very protective of them. At the first sign of rain, or a cold wind, they may steer them indoors. And as we all know, the DVD player can be a great friend.

In a school setting, we have the opportunity to redress that balance. We will probably have playing fields which are safe and protected. We have staff who are paid to spend time with the students and support them. Teachers are trained to spot danger and assess risk. Above all we can have flexibility with our curriculum.

Daniel, Ben, Ramzi, Usha and all the others benefit in important ways from spending time out of doors or doing some form of exercise. Daniel's anxiety can be lessened by a walk in the park; Ben's behaviour improves significantly after a morning's swimming; Usha doesn't want to be in her chair. She is happiest out of it, on the floor or better still out on the grass crawling around. For Ramzi swimming is such an integral part of his care plan that he goes three times per week.

Usha's friend Mary has a diagnosis of neuronal migration disorder. For Mary, movement, massage, physiotherapy, spending time in her standing frame, stretching her legs, sitting up on her knees, are not just add-ons, they are vital to her quality of life. They are her curriculum.

Apart from anything else, though, when a young person is as unrestrained as possible he or she will have so many more means of communicating. Strapped in a chair, Ben, or Usha, or Mary are restricted to pointing with their hands or eyes. Out of their chairs, or in the garden, they can communicate by moving about, changing their body shape, using legs as well as arms.

One of the best classrooms I have ever taken a group to was the local outdoor all-weather hockey pitch: 5000m² of nice soft Astroturf surrounded by a fence. We took 13 students, 10 staff, lashings of food and drink, and a whole minibus of equipment: balls, frisbees, tricycles, mats, parachutes.

We had a young man whose behaviour was so extreme that he was often restricted to one small 'soft' room. On hockey pitch days he would walk happily round and round the edge of the pitch, or run up and down between the goals. We estimated that he covered nearly two miles each time. His behaviour improved significantly after that.

We owe it to all young people with complex needs to give them the opportunity of spending as much time as possible out of doors. They have as much need for physical activity as the rest of us.

Sensory work

As we saw in Chapter 1, estimates of the numbers of young people with complex needs sometimes include those with what are often called 'multi-sensory impairments'. That is to say, they may have loss, partial loss or disturbance to some of their senses.

This is a very specialist area, and as with other specific medical issues will need to be assessed and evaluated by trained professionals before deciding if and how the school can begin to respond to these issues. Usha's friend Mary for instance has a visual impairment, and using light in ways recommended by professionals in this field may allow her to 'see' in a way that might be new and exciting for her.

The word 'sensory' is sometimes also applied to a whole curriculum for young people with complex needs. Many special schools are equipped with sensory rooms or dedicated classroom areas which can be blacked out and used for sensory work with light projectors, sound effects, tactile materials, etc. With these types of facilities and resourcing, young people like Ben, Ramzi and Kyle have the opportunity to explore the use of all their senses, and to be engaged in communication and response through touch, sight and sound. Our senses after all are what make us feel alive and aware, and for these young people effective sensory work, applied in a careful and appropriate way, should be a vital part of the curriculum.

As with all parts of the personalisation process, though, we must always be able to justify on a student-by-student basis why and how we use any sensory equipment. It is about making sure there is a real match between a student's needs and the use of a sensory resource as an aid to learning. Sometimes, a simple personalised 'sensory box' for each student can be as effective in the long run as a whole suite of expensive high-tech equipment.

So, not necessarily always a 'sensory' curriculum, but always a 'personalised' one.

In the next chapter we are going to look at how environment, staffing and timetable can be matched to the personalisation process.

Chapter 5

Environment, Staffing and Timetable

We are all sensitive to our environment, and young people with complex needs are almost certainly even more so. Creating the right environment for learning must be a priority, and by 'environment' I mean the colour of the walls, use of support staff, atmosphere, type of furniture, pace of lessons, access to assistive technologies and so on. Even the way we divide up the day – the timetable, transitions between sessions and managing personal care – will contribute to the environment we create for our young people.

The students themselves are also part of the environment. So I want to address the issue of whether students with complex needs should be integrated into classes with more able students.

Integration

Quite a senior member of staff at a special school I visited once, when asked whether children with complex needs were in a dedicated group or integrated into classes with more 'able' children, said rather tersely: 'We don't segregate here.'

The implication that 'segregation' is the opposite of 'integration' is a false one, because there are advantages and disadvantages to both approaches. In some circumstances young people with complex needs will learn better in a class of other young people with complex needs, and in other circumstances it may be more beneficial for them to integrate with more academically able students. It's not a black and white issue.

People tend to see this issue in terms of equality of opportunity, which of course is accurate, but just because a young person with complex needs is placed in a group of, say, young people with moderate learning difficulties, doesn't automatically mean he or she is going to receive the same attention and care, learn the same things as more able classmates. Be treated equally in fact.

By all means let's place Usha or Alice in a class of students who are significantly more able academically, or put Sammy and Kyle in a group of relatively high functioning autistic people. If they can still follow a personalised programme which suits them as individuals, then I'm all for it. In fact, all the other students in that class, irrespective of their ability, should have their individual needs met even if they are working towards quite high-level accredited qualifications.

To achieve this, though, we need to make absolutely sure that there is enough space, that support staff are adequately trained, that resources are appropriate, and that issues with behaviour can be addressed in such a way that the work of the rest of the class is not disrupted. That's quite a commitment.

Hillside Special School in Sudbury, Suffolk, in the UK has made that commitment. Hillside is a modern purpose-built school which has been judged to be 'outstanding' over many years by the Office for Standards in Education (Ofsted). I asked Deputy Head Gail Baxter what she feels the advantages are of an integrated approach:

> Here at Hillside we feel that integration provides those pupils with PMLD with a stimulating language-rich environment. The more verbal and more able pupils interact with the pupils with PMLD, and like to support them in their use of switches and other resources.

If the accommodation is fit for purpose, if the facilities, space, resources and appropriately trained staff are in place, then it is likely that the personal and learning needs of a young person with complex needs can be met in whatever class they happen to be placed, with added advantages for the rest of the school community.

Again, it's about being realistic. No matter how strong the arguments in favour of integration are, a school has to face facts: if it doesn't have the accommodation, resources and staffing to provide a personalised curriculum in integrated classes, then creating a dedicated PMLD group might well be the best outcome for the students.

A dedicated PMLD class must also be adequately staffed and resourced of course, but the main advantages of a dedicated group are that the needs of the students cannot be ignored, nor can any attendant safeguarding issues. The staff team will be trained and experienced in this type of work; they will have the time and commitment really to get to know each young person, and especially with older students staff will be able to act as advocates on their behalf as they move towards the end of their schooling.

'Dedicated' should never mean segregated. A dedicated class is a starting point. A base. An advocacy service. A place of safety where needs are met, staff have the time to get to know each young person, and the personalisation process can begin. If appropriate – and it usually will be – each student can then be timetabled at certain times of the week in other classes, or in sessions which reflect their interests and needs irrespective of the ability of the other members of that class.

Daniel, for instance, is only with the complex needs group for about half the week. He spends one whole day of each week on a community-based project with a group of people of his own age with moderate learning difficulties. He attends an art class with students who are not classified as having complex needs, and he is also integrated once a week into a numeracy class which reflects his interest and ability with numbers.

He is usually accompanied by one of the teaching assistants from the PMLD group – someone who knows him well and can ensure he is comfortable and that his needs are being met.

In Daniel's particular case, this is also someone who is experienced in dealing with his behaviour should he become overly anxious.

In the same way, one afternoon a week, Usha and Alice and Mary go to a 'girls' group' where they join girls from other classes and abilities in the school. They can do things and learn things which are age- and gender-appropriate and in no way dictated by their learning difficulty.

Nor should a dedicated PMLD class be an isolated class. The students should be as fully involved in the life of the school and have access to as many of the facilities, clubs and opportunities as every other student on the school roll.

We wouldn't expect any of the students in a special school to be isolated within their school community in the same way that we would not expect a special school to be isolated within its local community. In fact, some of the most successful models of integration happen in 'co-located' schools, where the special school is an integrated part of a whole campus, with maybe a secondary school, a college, and shared facilities such as sports fields, assembly halls, and even shared staff. In a system such as that it would hardly matter if the PMLD students were in a dedicated group or not, since the level of social integration takes places across the whole campus community on so many other important levels.

For the purposes of this book I am assuming that our students Daniel and Ben and Ramzi and Alice and Usha and Sammy and Kyle and the others are in a dedicated class of young people with complex needs. One of the implications of that is the question of how that group is constituted.

Groupings

Should we create discrete sub-groups, or whole classes, based on age, or will all students within the 14–19 years range be taught together? This is what Peter Imray says about the issue:

Why is age an arbiter of groupings? It seems to me that schools are the only institutions to sub-divide the population according to age and I'm really not sure why. Why are children (and ESPECIALLY those with learning difficulties) assumed automatically to have lots in common with their peers born between September 1st and August 31st, but no-one born outside of these dates? I may be alone in this but I do not check the birth dates of people before I become friends with them. My friends and acquaintances are generally sorted according to interest, compatibility, political / social opinions, relationship etc… but never age.

(Imray 2011)

As we all grow older, age matters less in social relationships. In any case, Ramzi learns differently from Ben, who learns differently from Usha in ways that have little or nothing to do with their age. The pace and progress of each student's learning is complex, unique and unpredictable. Their age is possibly the least significant factor.

It is not so important that a group is coherent in terms of age, but more that staffing, resources and environment can be flexible to meet the changing needs of the students. In one activity it might be appropriate for Ben, Alfie and Ramzi to work together, whilst for another Ben might be working on his own with a member of staff while Alfie and Ramzi join a group with Mary and Sammy. How this works in practice is of course a timetabling and staffing issue and we'll be looking at this more closely a little later on in this chapter. With possibly a high ratio of staff to students, it should be possible for the students to work in very small groups or even one-to-one for most of the week.

In fact, if timetable, rooming and staffing allow it, it may be that the whole group is hardly ever actually together. A full group may just be for meetings, celebrations and certain activities such as sport or relaxation which may lend themselves more easily to large-group work.

In any case, I prefer to see a class of young people as more than just a group or series of groups. What we have uniquely in a PMLD classroom, where the need to follow prescriptive national frameworks may be less, is the opportunity not so much to have a 'class' in any conventional sense, but rather to create an environment where the social dynamic and use of space allow the young people to experiment, experience and grow. More of a community than a classroom. Where students are as much a part of that community as the staff. Where the students help, contribute, get things out, put things away, support each other, water the plants, tidy up, and all and every task they can contribute to even in the smallest way.

The less pressure there is to follow an external curriculum or a prescribed system or approach, the more the student can be part of the life of the classroom community and of the school. It's a way of encouraging initiative and autonomy and is as good a preparation for life as anything. Of course Daniel won't mop up that water spilt on the table as quickly or efficiently as a member of staff. Sammy might actually make it worse, but the point is that at that moment where he is asked, where he reacts and engages, where he tries, he is exhibiting an independent response to a real-life event, and he is contributing to that community. And that's how we all learn and grow.

The first requirement for creating this kind of environment, an environment where young people can develop at their own pace, is to create as much space as possible, and for that space to be as calm as it can be.

Space

A large space will probably have a positive impact on behaviour simply because a young person with complex needs will feel less restricted. Daniel for instance will be able to walk and run around. Move from place to place. Find his own space. He will have choices and options about where he goes.

A young ambulant person with complex needs who has spent an entire school career in small conventional classrooms, where the space is defined by desks and hard chairs, may be displaying far more challenging behaviours by the age of 14 than students who have had the benefit of space.

Even the best designed special schools, though, are basically made up of 'classrooms' of various sizes. I'm not going to talk in square metres per person here, but what we should do is make whatever room we have as spacious as possible. First and foremost we need to accommodate wheelchairs, standing frames, hoists and beds comfortably. Not so that they are in the way, but so that they are a normal part of the environment.

After that, we need space for movement. Space which encourages independent thought and action. Space which is adaptable so that large or small groupings can be formed easily without having to shift furniture. Space where young people can find a quiet corner. Space where everyone can dance madly on a Friday afternoon. Some in chairs, some on the floor, and some on their feet.

Not just space restricted to the one designated PMLD classroom either. Young people with complex needs won't fully understand the conventions of the dedicated classroom, so why expect them to? The corridor can be an excellent environment for building independence, as we have already seen with Ben being given more or less free rein to wander the school while being shadowed by an attentive adult.

Similarly it's important to use other rooms in the school which are free during the day. With appropriate staffing, a group which seems too large for its designated room can be split across two rooms to allow for small-group and more personalised work. This is a timetabling issue, and we'll look at that later.

So what's the minimum amount of furniture we need in our designated classroom? A couple of tables? Possibly. Daniel enjoys sitting at a table in a quiet corner with a teacher aide, working on a laptop or tracing some shapes.

Chairs? Probably a few, but not all the same: a couple of hard-backed ones. A couple of comfortable grown-up ones. Maybe a jumbo beanbag or two. A more eclectic, mature environment. And carpet. These young people are big teenagers. They won't always want to sit on chairs, and why should they?

We need to use the furniture and space available to allow us to create a range of different modes and positions for our group:

sitting round a table, or in an informal circle, relaxing on the floor, eating, celebrating. It's all part of the learning process.

What else would we need?

Light and air. Natural light so that changes of daylight, weather and the seasons can be experienced in the room. High ceilings too, if possible, with plenty of windows that can be opened easily and safely. We're getting into the area of design here, and as we know, there's not a lot of money around at the moment for rebuilding schools, so let's stick to a fairly standard classroom.

A few low-wattage table lamps too, to light the classroom in a softer and calmer way. We choose to live that way at home a lot of the time, so perhaps we should try to re-create it a bit more in our classroom. It's all part of acknowledging the maturity of the young people we teach.

Music and sound too are simple and accessible ways of creating atmosphere. Ben in particular, Alice as well. Sammy and Kyle too. All are sensitive to the calming effect of some classical music. Group relaxation sessions are always enhanced with sound effects of water or the wind.

Resources

Resources for living are important too. Some basic equipment for practising life skills: a cooker, a fridge, a sink, maybe a kettle and toaster. These domestic appliances may have to be enhanced by the addition of assistive technologies, which can be an essential and liberating addition to the classroom environment.

Kirsty Soanes is an Assistive Technologist with experience of teaching young people with profound and multiple learning difficulties in the UK. I asked her about the role and place of assistive, or enabling, technologies in the PMLD classroom:

Enabling technologies help people activate and exercise control over their immediate environment and different aspects of their lives. These could be environmental controls such as switches linked to 'powerlinks', or switch interfaces which help people to perform tasks like boiling a kettle, accessing computer software, or turning on lights. There are also new and emerging creative technologies such as 'sound beam', or sound activated software which allow the user to paint and draw using their own vocalisations.

Good practice starts out with good initial assessment of need. And that will differ with individuals. It's about having a discussion as a group of professionals including the parents and support staff and always asking questions such as: what are the needs? Can they be met with technology? Should they be met with technology? Is technology really needed?

If there is something that technology can help with, that can't be met in any other way, once you get the right technology, once you've built trust with that technology, that can free that person in so many different ways.

As Kirsty points out, it's not about filling the classroom with expensive equipment for the sake of it. It's about carefully choosing technologies which will actually improve the quality of life of individual students.

Décor and wall space

The décor in the classroom needs to be considered too, especially if we are to create calming environments. Many of our young students – Kyle for instance, and Ramzi as well – find it hard to process too many visual messages coming off the walls. It may affect their concentration and their behaviour.

This is another area that Hillside Special School in Suffolk has thought about carefully. Deputy Head Gail Baxter sums up their approach to the décor of the school and choice of colours: '*We deliberately try to keep school less "busy", and only have simple large displays. On the walls we use muted colours, predominantly blues and magnolia.*'

Just because we are in a school, that doesn't mean that we have to cover the walls with posters, paintings, symbols and assorted objects. A nice calming colour wash on the walls can create a more appropriate, and certainly more mature, feeling in a PMLD classroom.

If there is room for displays of student work, though, it's important to be realistic and honest. We always need to ask who and what they are for. If Alice's response to an art lesson around the theme of 'winter' is to tip a pot of red paint onto a large sheet of paper and rub her hands round so that the paint spreads in a wild circle round the paper, then that's Alice's work. She has done it. She may recognise it for a while. It may give her a sense of self. So let's hang it on the wall and celebrate it.

If wall space really is limited, and personally I'd prefer lots of windows to lots of walls, it might be preferable to display each student's targets simply and clearly so that the whole staff team, and especially staff new to the class, can immediately engage in the learning process with the students.

Of course, resources have to be kept somewhere, which can lead to a lot of locked cupboards, which is a shame when we are trying to build independence and choice into the curriculum. If possible we should really only need to lock away those items which are either dangerous or fragile. To support the personalisation process, everything else can be kept in unlocked cupboards or in clear boxes. The classroom and everything in it is at least as much the students' as it is the teacher's. The young people should feel that most resources and all areas are accessible to them.

As with assistive technologies and displays, it's about being realistic and taking a 'less is more' approach. It's very easy as a teacher of students with complex needs to build up over a number of years an enormous quantity of resources. Some of these may be appropriate for a current student, and some will have been created for past students.

Maybe with resources it might be best to start off a year with a blank canvas. Just the absolute minimum equipment. Then, as we get to know the students, re-introduce those that are actually needed: some shape puzzles for Daniel, a drum for Ben, some clay or other tactile resource for Ramzi, a few large hard-backed picture books for Alice, a box of pens and paper for the student who is showing an interest in forming the first letter of his name. Things that the students can and will need and use. Things that will develop what they can already do. Boxes of small sensory objects, too, which can be personalised to each student. Things to touch and feel and shake and hear. As Gail Baxter at Hillside says: '*A simple selection of equipment so that it can be used appropriately and well – and on an individual basis.*'

If all the cupboards are open, and all the resources relevant and available, then there will almost always be something for each student to engage with. And what's more, it will have been the students themselves to some extent who have created the environment in which they work.

Of course, no matter how hard we try to make the environment as accessible and calm as possible, it is actually very hard for a PMLD environment to be consistently a calm place. There is just so much else going on. We've already seen that predictable and essential events like personal care or positional changes can and should be incorporated into the day as naturally as possible and never seen as a distraction. That's one good way of keeping things calm.

Nevertheless, any or all of the following, or more, can interrupt and contribute to increased noise, movement or stress: a phone ringing, staff absence, seizures, accidents, challenging behaviour, extreme weather, resources missing or not working, wheelchair breakdown, staff training, hoists not being charged, visits by therapists, nurses or other teachers, fire drills, whole-school events. The list goes on.

These events can only be predicted or minimised to a certain extent. The nature of special needs teaching, and teaching groups with complex needs in particular, make most of them inevitable at some time or another, often several within one day. The best we can do, I think, is to accept they will happen and manage them in such a way that they are seen as part and parcel of school or community life.

The staff team

We have already discussed in Chapter 4 some of the qualities needed to be an effective teacher in a PMLD environment. Qualities such as patience, knowing when to stand back, and knowing when to intervene. The need to be realistic and honest with yourself and with others. The ability if not to stay calm then at least to appear calm. A sense of humour goes a long way too.

It's an extremely stressful and difficult job. The strain of being responsible for some of the most challenging and vulnerable young people in our school systems should never be underestimated. Ros Ward has more than 30 years' experience working in special schools. She sums up the particular challenges of working with young people with complex needs:

> *I found working with a group of PMLD students was more tiring than other groups because if you are going to ensure they are learning and not just doing you have to be pro-active at all times. When working one-to-one you are either providing stimulus to provoke a response or observing intently, patiently waiting for a response and developing this. You are also responsible for the rest of the group ensuring they are actively engaged, making small steps towards independence, and safe. This responsibility for dedicated teachers and support staff is relentless.*

As Ros points out, there are very few down-times.

For a few seconds I once took my eye, and my mind, off Karl, the boy I described spending such a wonderfully 'free' hour with in Chapter 2. He set off, over the fence, along the path, onto the road and up the hill. I chased him for nearly a mile to the café which was his objective. He wanted a packet of crisps.

The teacher will almost certainly have to manage a large team of teaching assistants, teacher aides and support staff as well. They too will face the same stresses and challenges as the teacher. They do an extremely difficult job and yet they are probably not very well paid.

As people, they will be committed, hard-working and caring. Like the teacher, they will need to be realistic, flexible and resilient.

The way they respond to the students will not only impact on behaviour but will also create an environment for growth and learning.

Personal care is only one aspect of the teaching assistants' role. They too will get to know the students as individuals. In many ways, they will know each one better than anyone else in the school does, and because of this their input into planning, curriculum and decision making will be vital. They will have opinions, and it is important to listen to them.

It is the teacher's job to ensure every teaching assistant feels valued and empowered, that their skills and responsibilities are recognised, that their training needs are met, and that there is as much a commitment to their well-being as there is to the well-being of the students. Their work is mentally and physically exhausting. Many who have done this job for years have to retire early with back problems or other injuries. Allocated breaks during the day are vital and should never be forgotten or ignored. Nor should a teaching assistant, or teacher for that matter, ever feel ashamed about asking for help, or advice, or a few minutes away from the class.

Like the students, the support staff deserve to work in an environment where they are happy, feel they are part of a team but also have autonomy, and where communication with each other and the teacher is good. At least one meeting per week where the whole team can share, talk and offload will always make the learning environment more effective for all.

The key to making a personalised curriculum work is using the support staff effectively and involving them as fully as possible in teaching and learning. Which brings us to the timetable.

The timetable

The timetable is where the personalisation process can be expressed in concrete terms. It's not easy. It takes time to get it right; it's an ongoing process but it is worth it in the end.

Primarily, it's about timetabling the available staff and accommodation in such a way that the students are taught in small groups or one-to-one as often as possible. Let's take a hypothetical day. The very basic blank timetable looks like this:

Tutorial	Session 1	Break	Session 2	Lunch	Session 3	Session 4

We'll assume we are in a school here where it is accepted that beginnings and ends of lessons with a complex needs group can't be set in stone. So I'm not going to put in any timings. Daniel, Ben, Ramzi, Alice, Usha, Sammy and Kyle are all in this class. In fact for the purposes of this exercise they are the class. That's seven students, all with very different needs and abilities, and all with their own curriculum.

We can't possibly teach them all together all at once all in the same place. That just wouldn't work because this is a personalised curriculum and that means it's what each of them needs that matters. Unfortunately, we don't have seven different spaces, seven different members of staff, seven different bathrooms. What we have are seven students, three support staff, one teacher and one base room.

There are another couple of rooms free during the day. A music room in Session 1 and another classroom in Session 3. Also, the school field is quiet in Session 2. So now the timetable looks like this:

Tutorial	Session 1	Break	Session 2	Lunch	Session 3	Session 4
	Base Room		Base Room		Base Room	Base Room
	Music Room		Field		Classroom	

One teacher and three support staff. That's four people to support the seven students in one or two rooms or outdoors. The number of staff to students – a ratio of 4:7 – is hypothetical and perhaps a little lower than the average. 1:1 would be the ideal, but I am sure is very rare.

The simplest way to facilitate as much individual work as possible is like this:

	Session 1		Session 2		Session 3	Session 4
Tutorial	Base Room Daniel, Ben, Ramzi, Alice with two support staff	Break	Base Room Daniel, Ramzi, Alice, Usha, Sammy, Kyle with teacher and two support staff	Lunch	Base Room Ramzi, Alice, Usha, Kyle with two support staff	Base Room Daniel, Ben, Ramzi, Alice, Usha, Sammy, Kyle with teacher and three support staff
	Music Room Usha, Sammy, Kyle with teacher and one support staff		Field Ben, plus one support staff		Classroom Daniel, Ben, Sammy with teacher and one support staff	

Of course, in reality there will be complex social and behavioural issues to consider before finalising which student goes where and with whom. I'm not going to get into that here. This is just about how to ensure each student gets as much personalised attention as possible.

There will also be issues unique to each school, state or country system about whether or not support staff can lead sessions, even with very small groups. For the purposes of this exercise I am assuming two things: first that at least one member of the support staff team will be qualified to lead a small group provided the teacher has prepared the session beforehand. Second that all the support staff work regularly with these students and know them well enough to ensure that teaching and support is targeted and appropriate.

In Session 2, Daniel is able to access a higher level numeracy class elsewhere in the school, and Ben can join a particularly energetic sports group in Session 4. Both will be accompanied by a member of the staff team. So now the timetable looks like this:

	Session 1		Session 2		Session 3	Session 4
Tutorial	Base Room Daniel, Ben, Ramzi, Alice with two support staff	Break	Base Room Ramzi, Alice, Usha, Sammy, Kyle with teacher and one support staff	Lunch	Base Room Ramzi, Alice, Usha, Kyle with two support staff	Base Room Daniel, Ramzi, Alice, Usha, Sammy, Kyle with teacher and two support staff
	Music Room Usha, Sammy, Kyle with teacher and one support staff		Field Ben, plus one support staff Daniel plus one support staff to numeracy		Classroom Daniel, Ben, Sammy with teacher and one support staff	Ben plus one support staff to sports

Let's look at curriculum subjects. The framework for personalised work based on each student's targets and needs.

As we have seen in the previous chapter, some of these 'subjects'– Intensive Interaction and Sensory Work for instance – don't necessarily need discrete timetabled slots of their own provided the staff team is able to infuse the whole curriculum with opportunities for meaningful shared communication or for appropriate sensory experience. Best practice will probably ensure that this is the case, whilst identifying some specific times in the week for more targeted work in these areas.

The potential list of subjects is huge and likely to be increased still further if the school has bought into or had staff trained in specialist approaches such as Tacpac® (www.tacpac.co.uk), which combines touch and music to promote communication, or Soundabout (www.soundabout.org.uk), which promotes the use of music, sound and movement for young people with complex needs. Here are a few subjects which probably crop up on timetables for groups with complex needs the world over:

Communications	Community Trips	Tacpac®	Music
Intensive Interaction	Physiotherapy	Swimming	Life Skills
Relaxation	PSHE	Sensory Work	Food Tech.
Individual Target Work	Rambling	Horse Riding	Numeracy
Arts and Crafts	Occupational Therapy	Light Room	Alternative Therapies
	ICT	Sport	Soundabout

The choice of which are most relevant will depend on the needs of the group, the culture of the school, the skills and qualifications of the staff, and the availability of rooms, money and resources. The teacher will also have to make the choice about whether to timetable personal care or to allow it to take place as naturally as possible as and when it is needed. In either case, as I have said before, it needs to be treated as much part of the day as numeracy or lunch.

You may also have a curriculum theme – 'summer' for instance, 'the weather', or 'water'. These are fine as a means of focusing planning and providing variety for both students and staff. But again, whatever theme you choose, it will need to be flexible, open-ended, age-appropriate and never too rigorously applied. In a personalised curriculum, the student always comes first.

In our hypothetical instance here, based on just one day of the week, I am simply going to add some of the above to the timetable, as follows:

	Session 1		Session 2		Session 3	Session 4
Tutorial	Communication (Base Room) Daniel, Ben, Ramzi, Alice with two support staff	Break	Relaxation (Base Room) Ramzi, Alice, Usha, Sammy, Kyle with teacher and one support staff	Lunch	Food Tech. (Base Room) Ramzi, Alice, Usha, Kyle with two support staff	Individual Targets (Base Room) Daniel, Ramzi, Alice, Usha, Sammy, Kyle with teacher and two support staff
	Music and Dance (Music Room) Usha, Sammy, Kyle with teacher and one support staff		Physical Games (Field) Ben plus one support staff Daniel plus one support staff to Numeracy		Arts and Crafts (Classroom) Daniel, Ben, Sammy with teacher and one support staff	Physical Games Ben plus one support staff to Sports

The choice of subjects here is not wholly arbitrary. Some such as Music and Dance or Physical Games are dictated by the space available. Others are directed by student need: Ben has a huge amount of energy so two sessions out of doors on the field will be just right for him.

Session 2 in the base room poses a potential problem of staffing with a staff-to-student ratio of only 2:5. However, two of the students who present the greatest behavioural challenges are elsewhere being supervised 1:1, but it is still probably better to timetable a low-impact session such as relaxation at that point for the others.

This is the basic timetable. Within this structure, the teacher will where possible divide the smaller groups up further amongst the available staff and prepare activities and targets to be worked on in the session. For example, Communications in Session 1 could start with the whole group sitting in a circle for greetings. Following that, Ben and Ramzi could go to one part of the room to work on individual communication targets with the teaching assistant whilst Alice and Daniel work with the teacher in another.

This is a hypothetical and very basic exercise of timetabling. In any school and with any group of students there will be many other things to consider and many reasons why groups, staffing and accommodation will and won't work. What is important, though, that however carefully planned, however many hours spent on it, a timetable for a complex needs group can never be set in stone. Every day there are likely to be issues that will arise that will disrupt the very best laid plans, and staff have to be flexible enough to accommodate that. As we have said before, potentially everything is an opportunity for learning, whether it is on a formal timetable or not. Even the mechanics of the timetable itself, the changes between sessions for instance, present opportunities for music or other sensory cues, for the use of objects of reference, environmental cues, signing, touch, vocalisation or other forms of communication.

The timetable should be seen as an organic thing, being revised regularly throughout the year. Not only to allow all the students full and equal access to curriculum subjects over the course of a year, but also to give staff variety in their work. Students may work well with another student or a member of the staff team for a while, and then begin displaying challenging behaviours which can only be addressed by a change of activity, group or space.

In Session 4 of our hypothetical day, there is a session called 'Individual Targets'. Each student in a complex needs group will probably have a variety of targets which feed into his or her Education Plan, some long-term, some short-term, some generic and some skills-based.

In the next chapter we are going to look at how targets can be set and assessments made about the progress of individual students.

Chapter 6

Target-setting and Assessment

In this book I have suggested that to a certain extent young people with complex needs will learn and develop if they are given a level of autonomy within an environment with enough space and time for them to do things for themselves.

This is a non-linear, organic approach to their education. An education for life, where the focus is on creating an environment where they can learn at their own pace. An education where they are not constrained by external expectations, external curricula, external targets and assessments. An education where they are not held accountable against measurable criteria set by someone else. An education which is about each individual person.

It's difficult, though, to get away from some form of target-setting, so as teachers of young people with complex needs we have to learn to make targets work for us and, more importantly, for the young people we are working with.

Target-setting can be an important part of a personalised curriculum, not as an end in itself but as a way of providing guidance and signposts for everyone involved with the young person. Targets will allow the staff around the young person to stay focused on what is important for him or her.

The session on Individual Targets on our hypothetical timetable at the end of the previous chapter will be a time to make sure each student is getting the attention he or she deserves on the things that matter. If one of Kyle's targets is to walk from the classroom to the field without holding on to the teacher's arm, Session 4 on a Monday is a time when we will not be able to avoid addressing it, where there are no other distractions, and where that target and that target alone is the one thing that will matter for Kyle and the team around him.

For a young person with complex needs, targets are the link between what we know about him and what we hope he can achieve. They are a way of expressing that young person's curriculum – his unique and personalised curriculum – in terms of progress and development. They are the nearest thing you can get to a written curriculum, and as such provide one answer to the question: *'What do you actually teach them?'*

Of course, it would be stifling for staff and students to tie every moment of every day into addressing targets. It would be self-defeating because we would never have a chance to see the young person just as they are. And seeing each young person exactly as they are is where a good personalised education starts and ends. Nor would there would be any real opportunity for the young person to learn for themselves, to learn unexpectedly or in an unpredictable way, and all these ways of learning are vital for young people with complex needs.

When targets are good and effective, though, when they are personalised, they will sum up in a few words what is known about one particular student in one particular area at one particular time, and allow the team around that student to plan how he or she can be supported to move forward. Probably just a very small step forward. A step forward which may be followed by half a step back. A full step back even. But a step forward nevertheless.

Good and effective targets will be personal to each student. Unique.

I could try setting all the young people we are getting to know in this book the same useful real-life target – to butter a slice of bread for instance – but I'd be setting an almost impossible target for myself and the rest of the team.

Usha and Mary both suffer from forms of gastro-oesophageal reflux, which means that eating anything high in fat, even a slice of bread and butter, can cause them to vomit. Sitting at a table together, sharing a drink and 'chatting' with an adult might be a more realistic target for Usha and Mary in this kind of area.

Ben throws spoons and forks at the best of times, so giving him a knife may be unwise. Putting in place the appropriate type of plate and a plastic spoon and making sure his meal time is as calm and comfortable as possible may be a way of helping him to work on the more realistic target of holding his spoon for two minutes without throwing it.

Sammy can hold a knife and put it into the butter, but he prefers to spread the butter onto his arms and stomach. Buttering a slice of bread could possibly be a target for Sammy one day but right now a slice of bread is a target which is literally too small for him. Giving him a wax crayon and encouraging him to draw on an A2 piece of paper taped to the table may be a useful stepping stone.

Kyle is fascinated by the play of light on shiny objects. Being realistic, this is such an ingrained and probably unfathomable habit that it seems almost cruel to try to deny him it altogether. It is something which he really enjoys and is essentially harmless to him and others. We may just have to accept that for Kyle a shiny or colourful knife is just too interesting an object for him ever to be used for something as mundane as buttering bread. He probably has the fine motor skills to achieve it, but he prefers using these skills for changing CDs or playing a keyboard.

Since the operation to straighten her back, Alice has been far too busy enjoying the world in front of her eyes. She spent her entire life up to her operation looking at floors and table tops. Buttering a slice of bread requires just too much looking down for her new upright body. Walking to the cupboard and getting the loaf out, though – now that's a decent target for Alice.

Ramzi tends to interpret the world through his mouth anyway, so using bread and butter as part of a target might not be appropriate. Sharing a table with other students and not grabbing their food might be a good short-term target if backed up with enormous praise and congratulations.

So targets must be unique and useful to each individual student. They can be an end in themselves – buttering a slice of bread for instance – or a skill required on the journey towards buttering a slice of bread. They might overlap or be used in different combinations. Which type or combination of types of target used will depend on the young person and where he or she is at now.

Formal targets

As we discussed in Chapter 2, over the course of their lives each of our students will have amassed quite a few formal documents, most of which in one way or another assess their needs and abilities and often set targets for development. There's a list of some of these documents in Chapter 2.

Mary and Usha will have specific physiotherapy targets linked to their mobility, and Ramzi may have targets linked to his weight set by a dietitian. These specialist targets will have to be built into the planning process and into Mary's, Usha's and Ramzi's curricula. The document which defines a young person's learning difficulty may also contain targets which will need to be addressed and evaluated, as will targets drawn up in any formal education plan.

Even just taking into account 'formal' targets we are heading towards a very long list of targets indeed for each student here, and we don't want teachers, support staff and the students themselves to be overwhelmed. A personalised curriculum based solely on targets is likely to get in the way of the overall aim of fostering autonomy and independence.

So check formal targets and the documents they appear in carefully. Especially the date a report was written or formal targets set. Young people with complex needs tend to slip in and out from under the umbrella of different services. This could be for a variety of reasons including their age, the wishes of their parents, moving house or the changing policies of the state or national frameworks they come under. If a report which includes targets is more than a couple of years old, it might be advisable to contact the relevant authority for an update.

There will also almost certainly be some overlap or repetition even in formal targets set by different types of specialist agency. These are young people with complex needs, and with the exception of some of the specialist targets like those physiotherapy or dietary targets for Usha, Ramzi and Mary, it's that very complexity which can mean that targets from one agency may reflect or restate those from another. As an example of this, Sammy may have a target set in his sensory assessment which addresses his tendency to touch other people in inappropriate places. These issues could very well also be the subject of targets in his Behaviour Plan.

Informal or 'living' targets

Informal targets are part of the ongoing process of individualised learning for each young person. They are 'living' targets which truly reflect issues and needs which are relevant to the young person in that place at that time.

Living targets allow us to capture the moment when a young person engages with something, or nearly does something for himself. They encourage us to reflect on that moment and think about how the young person can be encouraged to move forward. This also means that each student has at least some targets which he has effectively initiated by his own actions or intentions.

Nadia is a 17-year-old girl who usually goes with her teacher to collect the register from the table outside the school office in the morning and then takes it back again once the teacher has filled it in. This is hardly an activity that will be relevant to her in her life outside school so doesn't seem on the surface to be something which could become a 'living' target in any way.

Nadia is a timid girl, though. Her parents do most things for her. At school she rarely acts independently, and always prefers to hold a teacher's hand, even for the shortest and simplest journeys round the school.

One of her formal targets, enshrined perhaps in her Individual Education Plan, could be 'to be more independent', but in a personalised curriculum, as we have seen in Chapter 4, every student will have the target to be more independent. If we are looking to keep the number of targets low, it seems almost a waste of a formal or 'living' target to say so.

A useful 'living' target for Nadia though might be:

- To collect and return the register to the desk outside the school office on her own.

The fact that it is the school register is hardly relevant. The 'on her own' bit is. It's also a target which is relevant to Nadia now in that it is useful to her and to her school environment, and relevant to Nadia's future as an invaluable step towards greater independence. It's a living target on many levels.

As with most targets, Nadia's achievement of this one will involve strategies and incremental steps as follows:

- For a few days she might carry on walking to the register table with the teacher as normal, with the teacher explaining to her that soon she will be doing this on her own.

- The teacher may then walk with her but explain that it isn't always necessary for Nadia to hold on to someone. The teacher can walk beside Nadia for a few days, then perhaps just behind her. Nadia may need a lot of encouragement and reassurance at this point.

- Once Nadia has shown that she is able to walk to the register table without holding the teacher's arm, the teacher may be able to stop and simply watch Nadia from a point where both Nadia and the teacher can see each other and be seen – the end of a corridor for instance.

The final point – when Nadia can leave the classroom independently, go to get the register and bring it back – may never be reached, but that actually doesn't matter. Nadia will have made small, significant steps towards, if not greater independence, then at least a feeling of what a little more independence might be like.

Stepping stones

Targets as stepping stones aren't always as clearly linked to an end point as Nadia's are in the example above. They will, however, represent the development of vital skills which contribute to the achievement of one or a number of other targets.

We've already seen earlier in the book how, for Ramzi, taking part in exercises like puzzles and shape games to improve his fine motor skills may allow him in the future to be able to put his shoes on completely independently. So if one of Ramzi's targets – formal or informal – is for instance 'to complete at least two shape puzzles once a day', that doesn't mean we are subjecting him to a pointless academic exercise. As Numeracy specialist Jane Barbrook said in Chapter 4 on the curriculum, we are teaching Ramzi and others primarily to '*develop their skills to solve practical and meaningful problems in a range of contexts*'.

Subject-specific targets

In the same way, subject-specific targets aren't necessarily out of place in a personalised curriculum.

We heard about Ben and his drum in Chapter 4. Ben has a target in music which reads as follows:

- To use his large drum appropriately at least once a day.

For Ben this will work on many different levels. It's a target specific to the music class on his timetable. It's a target which will help him find greater independence if we make it possible for him to get the drum himself. It's a target which is linked to improved communication if it is part of the process of using appropriate objects of reference or photo cues. It's also a target linked to his behaviour because Ben usually settles down well in class after using his drum at least once a day. It could also be that the music teacher sets even finer targets such as '*Ben will practise using one or two sticks.*' As a target, this will not only feed into his drumming but may also develop his coordination and ability to control smaller objects – like the knife for buttering bread for instance.

Experiential targets

I've mentioned before that 'experience' is also part and parcel of a broad and balanced curriculum and is a central part of the learning process for all young people with complex needs. Edward's father sums this up beautifully in our interview at the beginning of Chapter 8:

> *All we want is for him to be happy and contented and to have a reasonably interesting life. He is not that demanding as far as that's concerned. If he can have a few white knuckle rides and a few photographs and a couple of bottles of Coke then you would probably get a smile out of him.*

For some students, the school might be able to provide experiences which for all sorts of reasons their parents or carers cannot provide from home.

Alfie for instance, who we met in Chapter 4 playing with Ben's wheelchair, is from a large family and some of his brothers and sisters also have additional needs. His parents are very busy juggling the demands of everyday life with the care of their family. They do this very well but it does sometimes mean that they don't have time to take Alfie swimming – an activity which he loves and which makes him calmer. In this instance, a highly appropriate target for Alfie would be to go swimming twice a week.

We also met Aaron in Chapter 4. He's the boy who works at around UK National Curriculum Level P1(i) or P1(ii). Many of his targets are essentially 'experiential' simply because he is at the stage of experiencing the world around him from his chair or bed.

Aaron is tube-fed and taking in any liquids or solids through the mouth could be dangerous for him. However, the gastronomy specialist who works with Aaron and his family has recently said that he can begin to be allowed to taste different foods just on his lips. This can now become a target for Aaron: '*to taste one different thing every week*'. It's as valid as any other, and may be a wonderful new experience for him.

Many of these targets are short-term: Nadia's register target might just last a few weeks before she has gained the confidence to do the task herself. Some are long-term or ongoing: Ben's drum will probably not stop being part of his daily programme until he leaves school or loses interest. Some can be either. It really does depend on the moment, the task, the external circumstances and the young person.

For a young person with complex needs, targets, abilities, skills, competencies are all fluid. Organic. Sometimes a target is mastered more or less forever. Sometimes, it is mastered, forgotten, then mastered again. Sometimes, it is mastered, forgotten and never regained. It's why we have to treat these young people as unique individuals. They learn in unique and unpredictable ways. We will never do them justice if we assume their learning is a neat upwardly mobile progression through a series of easy targets.

Teaching groups of students like these is never an easy ride. There may never be a moment when we can tick all the boxes and move Ramzi, or Usha, or Ben onto the next level, because there isn't such a thing as a 'level'. There is just Ramzi, and Usha, and Ben. They will set the pace and the rules.

The question of how many targets one student can realistically have at any one time is a difficult one. As far as formal targets are concerned it's probably better to reduce them to as few as possible. Formal targets are likely to be around for as much a year, and be subject to scrutiny as to progress at regular intervals. The staff team will need to amass a body of pictorial evidence and witness statements which show the young person's progress towards the target. This is a complex and time-consuming business, so keeping to maybe three or four of them is in everyone's best interest.

As for other informal or 'living' targets, we can really allow them to have a life of their own. It's the only way we can ensure they are personal and relevant. As such there can be as many or as few as are relevant and useful at any one time.

It's not so much how many there are as what you actually do with them. They can be addressed at a specific time of the day, in a particular lesson, at lunchtime, at home time. They can be shared with parents or carers, escorts, helpers and drivers. They can be scribbled by a member of the staff team on a post-it note and stuck to a board, written into a lesson plan or just remembered and shared. They are literally an expression of what that student is doing now and what would be useful for her to do next.

Usha for instance is just beginning to get round to helping to wipe her own mouth after eating. If she can build on this it can be an important and relevant skill for her. It doesn't have to be written up, doesn't have to be part of a formal process or meeting, it doesn't even need to be measured, assessed and moderated. It just needs to be shared with lunchtime staff and the rest of the team.

Targets then are a convenient way of expressing a young person's curriculum. They provide an answer to the question: '*What do you actually teach them?*'

A target can also be a way of opening up imaginative and creative strategies for teaching and learning. People who work with pupils with complex needs tend to be not only patient and resilient, they are often creative and imaginative as well. So I am not going to spend much time on teaching strategies for addressing targets because everyone reading this book will be able to provide many more which are probably much better anyway. I am just going to consider a target which on the surface looks a bit dull and boring and may not seem to lend itself to a broad and eclectic approach:

- Alice will tolerate coactive movement with an attentive adult.

This one is about Alice's movement and linked to her physiotherapy assessment, but is also a way of addressing her nervousness and tendency to flinch and cry out when working with others. It's about her ability to trust those who are supporting her, and that is just about as important a living target as there can be for her future.

Here are a few ideas for strategies for addressing this target:

- Have an intensive interaction session focusing on movement in which an adult mirrors, echoes or copies Alice, no matter how small her movements may be.

- Film Alice for a few minutes interacting with an object or just moving her arms. Darken the room and replay the film on a large screen to give Alice the chance to watch herself, interact with the play of light on the screen, and move in ways which may be prompted by her own movement displayed in front of her.

- Go for a walk with Alice but let her lead. Follow where she wants to go, do what she wants to do. Support her only in the most minimal ways: opening doors she hasn't the strength to open herself. Keeping her safe.

- Sit with Alice at a table and give her access to some activities which are open-ended, such as using large bricks or shapes. Let her carry out the activities how she wants. Don't predict or model. Let your own 'play' be dictated by what Alice does.

- Ask a new or unfamiliar member of staff to spend some time with Alice. Just sitting with her. Keeping her own movements slow and gentle. Her voice quiet. Just allowing Alice to feel the presence of another person. Extend these periods of time every day.

- Sit next to Alice on a minibus trip. Allow your attention and gaze to be dictated by hers. Look at what she's looking at. Only occasionally point out things for yourself. Imagine she is taking you on a journey and is your guide.

Assessment

It's not easy to be specific about assessment because practices and procedures are likely to differ from school to school, state to state, country to country.

There may well be national indicators for assessing pupil attainment, such as the UK P-Levels, or other state or national standardised tests such as are used most commonly in the USA and also in New Zealand which you can use alongside P-Levels.

In many countries, however, particularly in Australia and also in the UK, older students with complex needs are assessed against their own goals as set out in an Individual Education Plan. This can be a more appropriate way of monitoring progress in the context of a personalised curriculum.

Broadly speaking, the only requirement is that their progress through a target is compared with where they were at the last assessment date. This is often expressed simply as a brief written report for each target. So that for instance if one of Ramzi's formal targets was '*to swim or take other forms of physical exercise at least once a day*', the end-of-period report might read something like this:

> *Ramzi has had a daily swimming session on his timetable for nearly a year. In general this has been successful except when Ramzi has been very reluctant to get changed and we have unfortunately been unable to persuade him to do so. On these occasions he doesn't seem motivated to do any form of exercise. It could be that he is bored with swimming. If this is the case, the staff team need to look at alternative exercise options for him.*

In the light of this report and Ramzi's changing response, the target might be revised for the following period to read: '*Ramzi will walk round the school grounds three times a week, and swim on the other two.*'

Another approach is to use some form of achievement continuum which records the extent to which the young person is able to carry out a particular target with autonomy. There are various models of achievement continuum, many of which will be known to readers of this book.

As an example, in the UK, the Qualifications and Curriculum Development Agency (QCDA), which is the non-regulatory part of the Qualifications and Curriculum Authority (QCA), has drawn up the following achievement continuum:

- *Encounter.* Characterised by presence and reflex responses.
- *Early awareness.* Characterised by fleeting attention and inconsistent responses.

- *Interest.* Characterised by more consistent and differentiated reactions.

- *Supported participation.* Characterised by co-operation and engagement.

- *Active involvement.* Characterised by recognition, anticipation and proactive responses.

- *Development.* Characterised by remembered responses and intentional communication.

- *Exploration.* Characterised by concentration, recall and observation.

- *Initiation.* Characterised by established responses and conventional communication.

- *Consolidation.* Characterised by the formation of skills, knowledge, concepts and understandings.

- *Application.* Characterised by the application of skills, knowledge, concepts and understandings.

(QCA 2009)

If one of Kyle's targets for instance is '*to choose his own snack in a café*', it may be possible over a period of time for him to move from 'early awareness', when he is made aware of the choices and perhaps focuses on a display of snacks, to supported participation, where he is able to pick a snack and carry it to the checkout.

At Granta School in Cambridgeshire, an achievement continuum is used routinely for target-setting with older students. As Head teacher Lucie Calow explains:

If a student has edged over from early awareness to the next continuum stage in some areas, a reasonable future target for him might be to cross that boundary in a number of other course areas.

Evidence

How can evidence of achievement be provided and validated when learning can take place anywhere and at any time, and is often unpredictable? John Carswell in Chapter 7 outlines some outstanding practice with photos, but they can also present problems in depicting reliable evidence of achievement.

A photo usually only shows a young person at a split second in time, taken from a particular angle in a particular place by a particular person. It can never accurately show the whole complex background to a young person's achievement. A photo of Sammy holding a paint brush over a piece of paper still has to be taken on trust as being a depiction of Sammy making progress in one of his targets.

Film too, though more likely to show a broader picture, is still only a slightly longer moment in time than a photo. It's also relatively time-consuming and resource-heavy. It may also not be appropriate for a number of reasons to film Kyle picking out a snack in a busy self-service restaurant.

In many ways it devalues the complex nature of learning for a young person with complex needs to reduce his learning to a moment in time. A snapshot. A few seconds of film. The 'evidencing' of achievement has to be, like so much else, an organic collaborative process based on dialogue and trust. The people who know the young person best – his teachers and support staff – are the best arbiters of his learning.

There has to be an ongoing honest and realistic dialogue amongst everyone who works with that person so that learning and target-setting can be constantly re-assessed and evaluated in the light of real experience. In many ways it is no more or less than an extension of the 'Getting to know you' stage described in Chapter 2. It's about re-examining our assumptions and expectations about a young person at a point in time and re-evaluating our teaching in the light of that process.

The issues here of course lie with consistency and accuracy. I suspect it is more common to overestimate the abilities and achievements of young people with complex needs than to underestimate them. Parents and carers can do this, and teachers and support staff as well.

This is usually for perfectly understandable reasons. We know the students, we want them to do well, and we like celebrating their achievements. We want to see that our efforts have paid off. This is so much part of human nature that sometimes we forget to be objective and realistic. We forget that Ramzi, and Usha, and Alice, and Karl and all the others will sometimes plateau, sometimes even go backwards for a short time. We forget that if they don't make the progress we expect or want them to make, it is probably not our fault. It's definitely not theirs. It's just how they are.

The added imperative of having to show progress through a linear model of assessment such as the UK National Curriculum P-Levels, or because we are told that a certain amount of progress must be seen to be made, can mean we feel even more pressure when making assessments.

There is a real role here for both internal and external moderation. Internal moderation generally means moderation carried out by someone else within the same school, and external moderation means progress being moderated by someone from outside. In either case, the moderator will need to see more than just a snapshot. He or she will need to spend a significant amount of time with each young person. Time in class and out, and at different times of the day. At the end of the period of observation he or she will be in a position to make a real and significant contribution to a discussion about progress made and next steps to take. Honest human dialogue based on time spent with each young person is the only really reliable way of making accurate and appropriate assessments of progress.

Finally, of course, there is another 'assessment' we all dread. Not so much an assessment of our students' progress – though that's usually part of it – but an assessment of our own abilities as teachers and of our own school's readiness to do the right thing by its students.

I am talking about the inspection of the school, its methods and its staff by an outside agency. These are scary events for teachers at the best of times, but often all the more scary for teachers of young people with complex needs because there is always the concern that inspection judgements will be based on the pedagogy and outcomes expected in a mainstream setting. There is also often the related fear that inspectors entering a complex needs setting will have no experience of special needs teaching and bring mainstream assumptions to the process.

In reality though, these fears are often groundless. In New Zealand for instance, although the Education Review Office does not specifically demarcate between the pedagogy of mainstream and special school teaching, normally at least one of the inspection team does have to have some knowledge of special needs.

In Australia, there are state-wide Teaching and Learning Audits which look at how a school is differentiating the curriculum for students with disabilities and special needs.

In the UK the Office for Standards in Education (Ofsted) is quite specific about its approach to inspecting special schools and their provision for students with more complex needs. When reporting on the quality of education provided in a school, inspectors must cover:

> *the extent to which the education provided by the school meets the needs of the range of pupils at the school, and in particular the needs of disabled pupils and those who have special educational needs (...) When judging achievement, inspectors must have regard for pupils' starting points and age, and the progress that the lowest attaining pupils are making.*

> (Ofsted 2012a)

This encourages an approach which allows individual starting points and progress made to be the primary considerations when looking at the education received by young people with complex needs.

There seems to be no need for teachers to be unduly worried about the progress their students are making compared with others, making the personalisation of the curriculum not only possible, but also inevitable:

For those groups of pupils whose cognitive ability is such that their attainment is unlikely ever to rise above 'low', the judgement on achievement should be based on an evaluation of the pupils' learning and progress relative to their starting points at particular ages, and any assessment measures held by the school. Evaluations should not take account of their attainment compared with national benchmarks.

(Ofsted 2012b)

The inspectors will also have to consider whether:

the (teaching) team has appropriate expertise for the range of pupils' needs (…) whether the physical environment enables all pupils to learn effectively, and whether learning activities and resources are age-appropriate and are different from those used in earlier years, even when pupils' attainment remains at low levels.

(Ofsted 2013)

'*Expertise, environment, activities and age-appropriate resources*' – all of which support a good personalised curriculum for young people with complex needs.

Head of Granta School Lucie Calow has also been an Ofsted inspector. I asked her what advice she would give to teachers of complex needs classes about school inspections:

I think that what a school needs, and what its teachers need, is a clear view about what constitutes good, satisfactory or outstanding progress for individual pupils and how they have come to that view.

Clarity is the key, and moderation (the process of being open to professional challenge and reconsideration) must be robust enough to be a valid tool for agreeing sound targets and outcomes.

I am not aware of an inspection system that would not accept clarity and robust moderation as reliable indicators of progress for older pupils with PMLD.

In terms of quality of teaching, clarity is also the key, and especially a shared clarity within the team accompanied by accurate and time efficient recording, pace of lessons and organisation.

The ethos of a classroom and how staff interact with and speak to and about their students is very important too.

In terms of behaviour management it's about all of the above. Are challenging behaviours avoided because of the skill of the staff? If they do occur unexpectedly, are they efficiently and respectfully managed? Is communication with the student maintained throughout the episode?

Here again, Ofsted is quite clear. Inspectors should consider:

how well the school supports its most behaviourally challenging pupils, even where there is only a small number, because many pupils with special educational needs require clear expectations, structures and systems, additional support to manage their behaviour, and robust arrangements to support their personal and social development.

(Ofsted 2013)

Having said all that, it's still a heart-stopping moment when things seem to be going wrong…

As we know, Ramzi used to have an issue with spitting. Quite a big issue. I had put in place a rudimentary three-stage system which I hoped would deal with this. Stage 1 was a response to his first spit of the day. It required the teacher simply to ask Ramzi as calmly and neutrally as possible to stop. Not sanction him, not exclude him. Just ask him nicely to stop. This system had been in place for about a week, when Her Majesty's Inspectors arrived…

The lead inspector came to my class and sat down. Pen and paper at the ready. She was hugely experienced, highly qualified, and very well dressed. Ramzi was sitting on his usual chair – a little bit apart from the rest of the group…and within spitting distance of the lead inspector.

With a dreadful inevitability he raised his head, pursed his lips and launched a gobbet of spit across the room. It landed on the perfectly pressed lapel of the lead inspector's jacket.

I realised that my career was over. I had allowed my pupil to assault one of Her Majesty's Inspectors in a most vile and offensive way. I was devastated. All I could do was mutter the appropriate stage 1 response: 'Ramzi, could you stop that, please.'

The inspector began to scribble earnestly on her paperwork. For me, I knew, this was the end. In fact, I'd done OK. The right thing in fact. The inspector had noted that Ramzi had challenging behaviour, that a system was in place to deal with it and that when the time came, the teacher had followed that system through.

The school did not receive a dry cleaning bill.

In the next chapter, we are going to look at options and issues for young people with complex needs when they are old enough to leave school.

Chapter 7

Moving On

The school leaving age for a young person with complex needs varies from country to country and from state to state. In Australia it is at age 17 or 18, in the UK it tends to be 19, and in New Zealand and the United States it is 21.

No matter what the age, though, leaving school and moving on to the next phase of life is a challenging time for a young person with complex needs. It's a challenging and emotional journey for parents and carers too.

Their son or daughter will probably have been in some kind of special school or special provision since the age of about three. They will have known where their child is from day to day and that they are in a specialist environment with trained and qualified teachers, therapists and support staff. The parents will have relied on the school for many years, and got to know the teachers and other staff far more closely than would normally happen in a mainstream setting.

To make things more difficult, the age at which the young person has to leave respite care, and the age he or she becomes an adult in the eyes of the Health and Social Services, may be different from the age at which they leave school.

When we become an adult in the eyes of the law, there is an expectation that we will speak for ourselves, make own decisions about the future. Be our own advocate. It is an assumption which of course should also apply to someone with special needs, except that more often than not, a young person with very complex needs will not be able to express themselves or understand the choices available to them.

This means that the last few years of a young person's education can be very unsettling indeed for parents and carers. Plans will have to be put in place early, questions asked, decisions made. It will be one of the most difficult and stressful times they will have faced in the life of their child.

From country to country, state to state, county to county, the provision, funding and choices available will vary enormously, but one thing which will be the same is that much of the hard work will fall on the parents or carers. They will become advocates for their sons and daughters like never before. There will be reports to be read, assessments to be made, forms to be filled in. It may feel like they are starting all over again. They will fight for funding, fight for the right services and support to be put in place, fight for their rights.

In many ways, parents will have to treat the transition of their son or daughter to the next phase of their life almost like a business, with budget plans, staffing and resources needing to be put into place, especially as funding may be coming from several different sources, such as Health, Education and Social Care.

Some schools will have a member of staff in place who is responsible for working with parents and carers during the last few years of their child's schooling, guiding them through the options available to them, the funding they may need to apply for and the paperwork that will need to be completed. They will go with them to colleges, respite centres, residential settings, day programmes and community groups. They will be a sounding board, a source of information, a shoulder to cry on.

Mandy Maass is Transitions Manager at The Edith Borthwick School. Her job is to oversee the transition of all the school's pupils to whatever provision may be appropriate for them once they leave. She sums up the challenges faced by carers as follows:

The parents and carers of young people with very complex needs
can spend years worrying about life beyond school, and also have the

responsibility of advocating for their young person, sometimes without obvious input. Typically, they will have fought for every bit of support to date, and sometimes the thought of new or different logistics and processes can be overwhelming.

I remind myself every day that we are dealing with real people and their lives. Sometimes parents and carers are too scared or proud to ask for support, or even ill-equipped to understand the importance of the decisions they are making. At school, the support for young people with profound and complex needs is holistic and immediate; carers want that in the future too, but the likely reality is that their young person will access provision put together like pieces from a jigsaw puzzle. The finished picture can be good, but the challenge is finding the right pieces and keeping them in place. As professionals, it's our job to support young people and their carers to reach this point.

Most parents will want their son or daughter to be able to continue with some kind of education provision for as long as possible. Here again, the provision varies widely.

One of the UK's leading providers of education provision for people aged 19–25 with complex needs is Chelmsford College in Essex. Their special provision was set up and is run by John Carswell. John is an Advanced Practitioner for learners with difficulties and disabilities and has over 25 years' experience working all over the UK with young people with profound and multiple learning difficulties. He was instrumental in bringing about legislative changes which allowed young people with complex needs to be educated within their own county or borough.

John describes the work he and his colleagues at Chelmsford College do for people aged 19–25 with severe and complex difficulties, and what he sees as best practice in this area.

Case study: Chelmsford College personalised learning programmes

The most important thing to start off with has to be the transition process from school into post-19 education. We try hard here to improve the quality of that transition by working in partnership with local schools. We visit as many special schools as we can and we invite the staff in those schools to come and see us. What's really useful as well is the Transition Brokerage Service offered by the local county. Each school has a nominated Transition Broker who is responsible for supporting the parents, the students, the carers and everybody involved with that individual. They are shown the opportunities for further education in their area.

At the same time there is a document called a Learning Disability Assessment (LDA) which all those people are invited to submit to. It covers medical needs, support needs, behaviour needs, education levels and outcomes, lifestyle needs, the learner's aspirations, likes and dislikes. Everything is captured in the LDA, and every student has one of these.

Once the LDA has been completed, I can then sit down, and put together a strong proposal for the further education plan for each individual student. We can cost it, we can predict staffing, we can look at support needs, medical needs, and we can look at training that we have to put in place in order to provide for that young person. Hopefully nothing is left by the wayside. It costs a lot of money so the funding package is normally quite robust.

That proposal will then go to County with a funding figure on the bottom, and once the funding has been agreed, we can offer the student a place at the college.

We currently have nearly 30 learners on our roll and each one attends college two days per week. We also have a small number of students who for one reason or another are unable to come to college, so we go to them and they follow their personalised learning programme from home.

For all our students, the information provided by their previous schools is invaluable. Everything that they leave school with is transferred over: their learning plans, information about self-help and living skills, behaviour plans. It would be awful to see any of those regress so as much as we can we incorporate all of that into their programme, into their learning.

All the good practice from the schools too with regard to communication is carried on. Picture exchange systems, signing, Makaton, assistive technology, photographs, symbol recognition, communication through body language. They will also receive a timetable system, like a daily planner, whether it be photographic, or switch-electric-based systems, or written, pictorial-image-based designed for them.

All of that good practice from school is still alive at college, which can be a great reassurance for parents and carers.

The first ten weeks they are at college are important, just to reassure us that they are at the level they are documented at from school, and to make sure that support plans are adequate and if I need to make any changes from their 1:1 support, 2:1 support. To make sure also that they are eating and drinking and their personal care issues are as documented.

We can then concentrate on the individual and in particular look at the things they would like to do as a vocation. When I use the word 'vocation', I mean what they are going to do for the rest of their life. That's where we start really.

We don't offer a curriculum here, though. That's one of the biggest advantages. Apart from providing an education which is broad and relevant, we are not constricted by any particular curriculum model.

We wait until the learner comes in to see what their curriculum might be, and what their curriculum wishes are. We then tailor an educational programme around their wishes. The curriculum is the learner's curriculum and nobody else's. It's not mine, it's theirs.

For example, if a young person likes working with animals, and that's something that they would like to do, then that's something that we'll start looking at. We'll look at activities that involve working with animals.

If they like cooking, if they like travelling, if they like sports or music we will put a programme together which includes those things. Not only that but if for instance when we go into sports it's a particular game, it's a particular way of accessing sport, whether it be watching, participating, listening to, whatever that is, that's the avenue we can go down, we can break it down.

We like to think that further education is a valuable tool to help them establish what they are going to do with their lives. This provision is for learners between 19 and 25, and they can spend 2–3 years here depending on their progress and depending on the funding options. It's a very important 2–3 years because this is their last shot with education. There is no option for higher education...yet. So this is it.

We have to have a high staff-to-student ratio. We're minimum of 1:1 and most of the time we are more than 1:1 because we have to have 2:1 support when we access community, for safety reasons and so on. For all personal care that involves manual handling it's 2:1, and for lifting and repositioning it is 2:1. Some learners with behavioural difficulties require 2:1 support, and even on occasions 3:1. All those staffing needs go into the LDA too. So that's a very large staff team.

The team is made up of specialist teachers and specialist support assistants. People with training specific to people with profound and complex difficulties. They are qualified in things like speech and language therapy, occupational therapy, behaviour management techniques, etc., so that we can reassure parents and carers that all the targets they had in school will be carried through and integrated into their programme.

Our facilities include a number of rooms, classrooms and base rooms that are designed to meet the needs of the learner: hoisting for lifting handling, sensory areas, and soft furnishings. There's lots of space and it's all at ground level and accessible because we need to reflect the school environments where they have just spent possibly 14–16 years.

So as well as supporting their needs we are able to provide consistency and also give parents and carers some reassurance, because coming to a big mainstream college for the first time can be quite scary.

A lot of the learning is community-based as well. We are looking at things they want to do with their life, activities they are going to do, so obviously we access the community an awful lot too. We have a student currently who loves trains, so we have an arrangement with a local station that he can go there once a week with two support staff to do some train spotting. He loves it, and it's something we hope he can continue with when he has left college. It's a vocation for him, and a very important one.

Our focus here is on continual assessment. The student's targets are monitored throughout the day through our learning plan system, and we capture every single outcome that is related to their targets. We put handwritten notes on their target sheets throughout the day.

In addition, each learner has a camera which goes with them wherever they are, and they are photographed throughout the day, as they work on their targets. The parents sign agreements that cameras will be used all the way through the programme, in the community and everywhere else. If we go to certain community venues we seek permission to take photographs there.

The staff have training in capturing action photos, because one of the dangers of photographic recording is that it's too posed. So the staff are guided all the time to capture real photos which represent the progress and the outcome as much as we can, and those photographs are used on their learning plan.

The students themselves use those photographs in their photographic diaries, so they are recording their learning themselves. At the end of every day we print the photographs and put them in their diaries. It helps the learners celebrate their achievements too, especially if we show the photographs on large screens.

We also submit those diaries to accreditation bodies, and we can then reference them to the accreditation criteria so that students are also gaining certificates of achievement and other qualifications. We don't teach to accreditation criteria, we show the accrediting bodies what our students have been doing and ask them to come up with ways of accrediting those achievements, rather than the other way round. That's very important.

As for our students being integrated with the college itself, there has been a provision here for people with mild and moderate learning difficulties for a number of years, but since we arrived three years ago there is a presence of learners with profound difficulties as well, so now there are students often being escorted through the college 2:1, using wheelchairs with all sorts of breathing machines attached, and being escorted by nurses.

So now every student at the college, whatever their level and programme of study, has a section included in their induction programme to raise awareness of the type of learners we now have here. It's also made quite clear to them that there is an acceptance policy and zero tolerance for bullying.

We also run professional development staff training weeks, aimed at all college staff, to raise awareness of working with and supporting people with profound difficulties.

It's actually really nice when we have new parents and prospective students visit us and there are hundreds and hundreds of students from all sorts of areas just walking around and they feel very, very comfortable, it's quite a nice surprise for them.

One of our goals here is that even before they have left us, they will have a nice package of vocational activities as their destination. So as they go through their 2–3 years with us, their vocational activities become more and more.

What we say to the families and the students is that when you finish at college, our hope is that you won't be in the same situation as you were when you left school. You will already be involved in a programme of vocational activities as your destination.

So, for example, one particular learner might be going to his local farm as part of his college programme. He helps feed the chickens, does some litter picking and emptying the wheelbarrows.

If he likes this and he is learning and he's received accreditation for this learning we may be able to move that activity whilst he is still at college into one of the other days of the week when he is not at college.

It then may become a permanent activity that he could do for many, many years, especially if we have built up a good relationship with the farm itself. It probably won't be paid work, but for the student it will be a vocation.

We also find that by personalising their education, by allowing them to do the things they would like to do, their behaviours improve, their health improves, their motivation levels are higher, and their anxieties are lower.

As well as an educational provision for their son or daughter, one of the hardest long-term decisions the parent of a young person with complex needs will have to make as they grow older is whether their son or daughter will live with them or whether they will try to find some sort of assisted independent accommodation.

Sammy, one of the young people we have been getting to know throughout this book, now lives an independent, but supported, life in his own home. I interviewed Sammy's parents Chris and Sherree about this:

Case study: Sammy's story

Sammy has just turned 21 years old and for the last three years nearly he has been living in a two-bedroomed house that he rents. He lives alone with a team of carers, one of whom is his older brother Bobby. The accommodation is within five minutes of us by car. He's settled in there extremely well and it has done so much for his confidence and independence.

His brother encourages him to clean away his own dishes at meal times, to use the vacuum cleaner, make his bed, and he's started choosing his own clothes to wear in the morning.

He does things now before he is told to. He anticipates what he is going to be asked. Even when he comes to see us he will take his plate to the kitchen and scrape it, rather than chucking the whole plate and knife and fork in the dustbin, which is what he used to do before.

He loves having his own home. Whenever he stays with us he very quickly puts his shoes and socks on when Bobby comes to collect him, and off he goes.

Before he moved into his own place he had spent six years in a residential care home but when he turned 18 he had to leave there and look for other alternatives.

First of all we thought that he might go into a young adults care home but unfortunately there was no place available for him. Also they did say that if Sam had been an aggressive sort of person he would have been able to be placed in shared housing or a residential place, but because he's not aggressive in any way there were no placements for him, so that's another reason we went the route of finding his own place really. He could have come home and lived with us but our preferred option was to try to get him his own place along with 24-hour care.

We were actually kind of pioneers with this. Some of the first people to go down this route. Sammy's social worker helped us a great deal, and the local authority were very open to giving him a personal budget in order for him to live on his own.

We had to put together a personal care plan involving all sorts of detail like what activities he is planning to take part in, and we had to calculate the cost of 24-hour care. We had some specialist help with that from a local organisation which assists disabled people.

Before doing all that, though, we had to actually find him somewhere to live because personal budgets are given to people who live in their own accommodation. They don't apply to young adults who live with their parents at home. Luckily we found somewhere for him to rent quite quickly, and then we applied for housing benefit as well.

Of course, one of the things is that you have to supply your own staff, which was very worrying at the time. We've been very lucky, though, to find the staff that we have got because they've been friends or people who have worked with disabled people. He'll always have that 24-hour care.

It was just a hard decision all round really, but we think we made the right decision for him. He doesn't talk and say whether something's right or wrong so we have to go on what we feel is right for him.

Sam wouldn't really want to be with us 24/7. We wanted to give him his own independence and we felt that he would probably develop more and also he would be able to make a wider circle of friends in the community if he were living by himself rather than with us, and that has proved to be the case. He has a very wide circle of people he's in touch with and he thoroughly enjoys the independence that he has got as a result of that. He's come along so much.

He's a lot calmer and a lot more confident as a person. He'll tackle virtually anything really.

There's silly little things that we've noticed a huge improvement in. Like before, he wouldn't go near a dog or a cat or a horse. Now he strokes cats, and horses.

In fact with college he actually works at a stables. He's got a routine there that he follows and he's got his own tasks that he does and he uses his own initiative as well. They go to the stables and he knows that when they get off their bus and go in, he has to go and get a wheelbarrow and start clearing and he actually walks in on his own and goes and gets the wheelbarrow and starts his work. He mucks out the stables.

Yes, getting him his own place was the right decision. We were dreading it at first of course. The emotional side of it was hard. Because of letting him go. There were a lot of tears.

The only thing that we could console ourselves with was the fact that if it didn't work he could come home, but you've got to give it a chance and we did, and we think we made the right decision.

From the wider family point of view it's been good too. His brother Bobby encourages the family to go and visit him, stay for tea or a meal. All the grandchildren have accepted him much more than when he was just living with us. They see him as a person now, an individual.

We get asked down for tea too of course. Or we go and have a meal with him. Sam likes to show us round and he lays the table. I think he just enjoys showing people where he lives and his bedroom, and what he's got.

So, yes, it's been very positive for him, and for the whole family circle.

There's a lot of love around him.

So that's Sammy. In the final chapter we are going to get to know one more young person and see how we can apply some of the ideas discussed in this book to his personalised curriculum.

Chapter 8

Edward's Story

We've met Edward a couple of times before in this book. We know already that he has epilepsy, that he gets on well with Ramzi, and that he likes flicking laminated symbols across the room.

For the final chapter of this book, I want to look briefly at how the personalisation process we have discussed in earlier chapters might be used to create a unique curriculum for Edward.

Of course, we all need to get to know Edward a bit better first. So I sat down with his dad, Paul, and asked him to tell me about his son. Paul and the rest of Edward's family agreed for the following edited transcript of our interview to be reproduced here.

Tell me a bit about Edward. What's he like as a person?
I think that Edward is generally a fairly happy and contented lad at the moment. He doesn't speak, but he is able to communicate quite well with people in different ways. He has got this fantastic smile that seems to charm people and enables him to get away with an awful lot! He can be pretty demanding at times depending on the cycle of his seizures, whether he is leading up to one or whether he has had one, which can make him feel a bit grumpy. He has certain obsessions and things that he wants and he is very single-minded sometimes. We find it hard at times to deal with him. He has this thing about butter and this thing about Coca Cola and it's hard to divert him. He loves photographs. He likes to look at the image but he also likes to flick them through the

air. He likes to see the movement of things through the air. He's always liked that. Generally, when he comes home – which is a couple of nights a week – as long as he's got some photographs and a bottle of Coke and a bit of attention, he's a happy boy.

I think that in some ways he's quite sensitive, although it is not always obvious. When things change and there is a different pattern to when he is coming home, for example, or if other members of the family are there, he can sometimes get quite embarrassed. And sometimes he doesn't know how to cope with that and he might grab you or pinch you or whatever but it's just because he wasn't expecting it. So we've always had to try to pre-empt what we are going to do and try and explain things to him ahead of it happening. I think he does understand quite a lot.

What was he like as a baby?
Well, as far as we can remember he was just a normal lovely little boy. We had had our daughter before and so I suppose we had gone through the whole process and knew what to expect. In the early months of his life he was actually saying a few words. That's a sad thing to think back to. He was saying some of the baby words that you would expect young babies to, but that just went altogether, it just disappeared. I can't remember exactly when. Now there is very little apart from him saying 'hello' and possibly 'no' and maybe, just about, 'home'. He had his first seizure after he was about three months old, and it lasted for 20 minutes, and obviously it was pretty terrifying at the time. We were preparing to go and see my parents in Zimbabwe; the doctors thought it was a febrile convulsion and convinced us to go anyway. He had his second seizure three weeks later in Zimbabwe, which was not the greatest place to test the health system at that time. And he had a further seizure on the plane coming home, so the GP referred Edward to a paediatrician and we started the whole process of him going on all these different drugs. We have built up a good relationship with the paediatrician over the years, but I suppose we started to realise that a paediatrician isn't a god. We had to agree with everything they said, though we began to realise that the permutations of the drugs were largely a bit of trial and error. I can remember, for example, that he was on one particular drug,

and we took him on a holiday in Cornwall and it made him sick up all the time, it just didn't work.

I also remember that when he was about two and a half, Great Ormond Street suggested something called a ketogenic diet. It's something to do with controlling the level of ketones in your bloodstream. It was supposed to reduce the number of fits and I think it did have a positive impact but I think the price we paid was just too high. The diet involved a high level of fat intake and a low level of carbohydrates. We literally measured and weighed everything he ate and everything was piled with lots of salad cream and butter and that sort of stuff. You felt rather sorry for him because as a treat he would have small packets of little carrots. You know, as if they were like sweets. We're not sure but that's perhaps one of the reasons why he really does love butter. It wouldn't be something that we could do with him now, he just wouldn't put up with it.

So over a period of time we gradually got the right balance of drugs but in his early life we were calling the ambulance and he was going in to hospital roughly every two weeks. So it was quite a strain on us as a family. He was being admitted to hospital but the typical pattern was that he would then wake up the next day and he would be largely fine after he slept it off.

We've had two occasions, though, where he nearly died, the fits were so long. I remember one occasion when we went into hospital and he was surrounded by so many people – fourteen, I think – it was frightening. In the end they had to rush him into Great Ormond Street. We were given accommodation there and we were just getting off to sleep and they rang us. Up we went into this intensive care and there he was standing there smiling as if nothing had happened. So, it was tough. He was in and out of hospital on a regular basis.

You do remember those times very clearly. For instance, he never liked things on him, but they always had a cannula in his arm when he went to sleep after a fit. I would be falling asleep on the bed next to him and he would wake up from the fit, rip the cannula out, and then blood was spurting everywhere and I would wake up. It was certainly interesting!

Apart from his epilepsy, at what stage did you first notice he might not be developing in the same way as other children of a similar age?

I think that it is very difficult to pin down exactly when. To be honest I can't really remember when we started to see him doing the flapping of his hands which is one of the signs that he had other issues. In some ways we sort of knew that there was something else there as well as the epilepsy but it wasn't until we had actually been to Great Ormond Street quite a few times. It wasn't until he was about eleven when we went to Great Ormond Street and I will always remember, we were sitting in a room and the consultant had all his acolytes behind and we sort of walked Edward in and it was within literally seconds that he said, 'Edward is autistic.' No one I think, up to that point, had actually made that diagnosis and actually said it. They talked about it, but it was partly due to the system and not wanting to make assumptions. When you start to label kids with this sort of thing it equates to costs and other factors I suppose. But to some extent it was a bit of a relief.

He had always been at a special school, though. We were very fortunate because obviously until we had a child with a disability we were not even aware that there was a special school nearby. We were very pleased to find that it was very close to where we lived. A school with the sort of skills and expertise that it has. Luckily it is still there, which is a whole other subject for me. Certainly I think that it is very important that you have schools with all this specialist expertise. They can provide the service that the parents need for these sorts of children with these complicated disabilities. I think that also, unlike a lot of parents, we did actually accept his condition fairly quickly. I suppose it was pretty obvious to us that he was going to have a big problem in his life and it was going to be difficult.

We also realised the need for us to have some sort of a break. So we managed to push for that quite quickly, and people would come round and stay at our house for a certain number of hours. We would then be able to go off and do something.

As well as that, we were able to get some respite where he would go and stay somewhere else, which was, again, very hard. On the one hand, first of all accepting that was what we were going to do but then fighting to get it. You had this double issue.

First of all you go through all the emotional turmoil to accept what you are going to do and then you finally do it, so you have the two battles. Your own internal battle and your second battle with the authorities, but we did decide that we wanted to have a bit of time to ourselves and for our daughter.

We started to take him to a respite centre. We always remember that when we first visited, it was a daunting place, it seemed like you would go to the front door and there were all these kids, you know, it just seemed a bit wild and not a lot of control. I suppose we hadn't got used to seeing kids like that, kids that we are used to now at school and at the activity centre he attends. We can cope with it, but at the time it was quite frightening, for us and for our daughter, but we did it and Edward stayed there and they did a good job, but it was hard, it was tough and I think that there are an awful lot of parents who don't accept it, particularly if it is not quite as obvious as it was with Edward.

As he got older how has he changed?
I suppose again, it isn't easy to see because it's so incremental, it's like any child if they are with you all the time, you just see this gradual change. I suppose that first of all is the fact that we managed to get the drugs and his epilepsy under control. That was a good thing. We managed to stop going to hospital every two weeks. In his development we have had difficult times and one of the big things that we thought we would never achieve, at one point, was to get him out of nappies. We just thought that it would never happen. That he would actually understand what he was supposed to do, and when. That was a big factor for us. I can't remember exactly how old he was. It was gradual. School had a big factor to play in it and just getting him used to a routine, trying to do it and understand it and what was needed. So that was one.

Also there was a time when he was doing a lot of spitting if he was unhappy, which was quite often, and you could sense his frustration and he couldn't explain to people what he wanted and so it was just an easy way of reacting. So over time I suppose he has, thankfully, got better, he's calmed down a bit. His fits have not been as frequent, but it's taken years. At school everybody there really understands him and I think it's another factor that there is that continuity. There are a lot of teachers in his school that know him and have seen him grow and develop and have been there all the way through, most of his life. So that's been good. He knows where he is going.

What has been the effect over the years on your family of having a son with complex needs?

Well, it has been very stressful and it has been a battle. I think my wife and I have worked effectively as a team to get the support and everything that we need. My wife is very good at understanding all the different facilities and everything that is available and frankly she gets upset at times. I'm better at talking to people and reasoning with people. But I suppose what stands out is that you have a child with a disability and you get over that shock but then you don't have somebody who comes along and says, 'Well, we're very sorry about this but we are here to help, and this is the range of facilities and services that we can provide.' It's not like that. So you just have to find out for yourself and you work by talking to other people who have gone through the same experience as you, working with the school, and gradually build up a network of contacts and links to establish what you can and can't get. Initially we were very reluctant to take any of the state benefits, but as the years went by we thought, 'Well, why shouldn't we?' It benefits everybody.

Getting him into full-time respite was very traumatic and such a struggle. The only way you could get there was by almost coming to the point of breakdown. That's rather unfortunate. You have to get to that stage first.

We had a daughter who was, to some extent, being left out, especially when you had an obvious medical situation which needed immediate attention. She was only five or six when he was born and she was quite young when we started to have issues with him, and he started having fits, and it was pretty frightening. Now of course we are used to it and so is his sister. Which is great, which has been good from her point of view in that sense in that it's opened up her eyes to a whole different world. I'm not saying it's something we would wish on anybody but it's certainly broadened her outlook on life and she has been a fantastic asset in helping us deal with Edward. It's hard to see a benefit in these sort of situations, but she's gone on to work with children with disabilities and I think it's enabled her to have a broader view on life and to cope with situations without getting panicky. She's quite a resourceful person.

The wider family have helped where they could but everybody's got such busy lives so we have never really depended on anybody else. They've come to see Edward and we have tried to keep in touch with them as best we can, and I suppose it is something that does upset me a bit, that because he is not at some of the family social functions, you sometimes think is he forgotten.

So, we've got through it and possibly we are a stronger family unit as a result of it. I know for some it is too much and there are a lot of marital breakups because people can't cope with the whole situation, but we've got through it.

Do you think having Edward as a son has had an effect on your social and professional lives?

Well, I think it has made it pretty demanding. Certainly when he was younger and living at home, we were spending lots of time looking after him, caring for him and dealing with the issues and dealing with the fits and it becomes pretty wearing over and above your everyday workload. Particularly when I was commuting up and down to London, so yes it does have a stress and a strain on it but, as I said earlier, we managed to get some respite. I had a good job and a company that was understanding, so they didn't have a problem with me dropping everything and shooting off to support my wife Lesley when he was having a fit and being admitted to hospital. But it was difficult and I was lucky. I think that it would be more difficult now, in the current economic climate.

I suppose we also got to know people, though, who had similar children, with similar problems and we got involved in groups to try and support those. I was a governor at his school for a bit, and I was involved with PARC – a local activity centre – for many years, so we would try to help people who were involved in that. We met other people and did start to realise how many people are out there with problems of one sort or another and need some support. But it would put more stresses and strains on you.

What have been the challenges you have faced getting him the support and education you think he deserves?

It has been a steep learning curve for us both and I think that we were fortunate to work together as a team, my wife and I, to actually work the system and to find out where we could get help for him and to challenge people and ask for these different facilities. I think that it is an unfair system, there is no booklet or group of people that come out and say 'we can help you in this way or that way'. You have to discover it all for yourself. His school have been fantastic from day one and they always try to help us and point us in the right direction, but you obviously see situations where families break up, and it's a single parent and that parent is so focused and stressed by just looking after the child that they don't really have time to educate themselves in terms of going on the internet, finding out what's available, going to see all the different authorities. So I think obviously it does help if you are reasonably articulate if you make a case and push for what you should have. And that's the sad fact of it.

I think we did fairly well up until the point where we just felt that we couldn't actually continue with Edward living at home any more. He was about 12 or 13. He was getting physically quite big, and if he didn't want to do something it was very difficult to deal with him. I was working full-time and it just got out of hand really.

Having gone through the emotional strain of making that decision, which was pretty awful, we thought that he should go and live somewhere else, and then you have the secondary factor of actually having to try and get him into somewhere. Of course, you want it to be local, you don't want it to be miles away.

So we were lucky to get him into where he is now but it was clearly not going to be easy because it must be very expensive, bearing in mind that it's 24-hour care, and Edward should really have pretty much a one-to-one most of the time and you've got people in shifts, coming and going. I can understand that they are not going to give that sort of facility out easily. But I think you do have to get to the point when you really are close to a breakdown situation.

And to be fair, where he has gone has been excellent. A lot of the people there have worked there for many years and it is a real vocation for them.

So, yes, we were delighted when we found that the school was on our doorstep, and the respite centre not far away. But then you do sometimes sit back and think, well we happen to live here, but at some time we might move and are the facilities for children with special needs going to be better in Cornwall or Yorkshire or different parts of the UK, and then obviously you think beyond that, is it better in Sweden, Denmark or America?

What are your hopes for Edward for the future?
Well, he is going to be 18 soon, and we know that he has to move out of where he is living as he becomes an adult and this creates changes in terms of his social workers, in terms of when he goes to hospital, because you are then an adult. Which is quite stressful.

Basically we have started to look around at where he could go. We are hoping that he can continue at his special school for another two years. So we can move him from where he is living first, and then worry about when he moves away from school. It's sort of in stages.

We are lucky that he can carry on at school for a couple more years, but basically, I don't think special schools should be run on the same basis as mainstream schools, in terms of their timetable, and how long the kids go there. As far as I'm concerned kids with special needs should be there probably until they are nearly thirty. And you shouldn't have big holidays in the summer and all this sort of stuff because they forget things and it's stress on the parents because they have to find somewhere where their kids can go for six to eight weeks. It's still a problem even now with Edward.

We have this idea that he needs to be in more of a community. We are really concerned about his short, medium and long term future so we are looking both in terms of the next few years but also how is he going to be looked after when we are no longer here and how we are going to make sure that he is not a burden on my daughter because she is going to have her own life to lead. We haven't got any other children, we've just got our daughter and why should she take on all the responsibility? So we were looking at something that there is not a lot of, in other words a bigger facility with a community with an overriding organisation that is going to be there in the long term. When you look at the individual privately run homes, and there are some very good ones, they all look fine, but you think what happens when the couple that are running it decide that they want to retire, sell the houses? That is a real concern.

We don't necessarily want to go back to the idea of institutions, though, people living away from mainstream society. I remember going to visit this one place, and the first thing I saw when we got there was a very attractive Victorian building and it had this old stone crest on it which said 'Epileptic Colony' and you think, 'Is that how they thought of it?' It was like keeping them away from everybody else. It must have been awful.

I know that there has been all this discussion over recent years about integration and being part of mainstream society but I think sometimes you have to accept that you need sufficient numbers of people, the expertise, and people to live in, and give that support. It's getting the balance really.

We accept that he is never going to have a job, and that he is going to need to be cared for, for the rest of his life. All we want is for him to be happy and contented and to have a reasonably interesting life. He is not that demanding as far as that's concerned. If he can have a few white-knuckle rides and a few photographs and a couple of bottles of Coke then you would probably get a smile out of him.

A curriculum for Edward

As Paul says, Edward is now 18 years old. He is an adult in age and in size. Initiatives which were tried out on Edward when he was much smaller, like the ketogenic diet, he just won't put up with any more. Like many 18-year-olds, he is strong-willed, and knows what he does and doesn't want. He is a reluctant participant in lessons.

We need to accept that, and look at a more age-appropriate and personalised curriculum for Edward.

Edward exhibits a range of behaviours, some of which could be called simply awkward to manage and some more challenging. At the less challenging end of the spectrum, he enjoys throwing plastic bricks into boxes, and flicking photos or laminated symbols around the room – something he does with remarkable accuracy at times.

Flicking photos and throwing bricks into a box is something Edward does. It is a very typical Edward activity and doesn't really cause anybody any harm. After a particularly enthusiastic session there will be photos strewn all over the floor, but that's about it.

His more challenging behaviour is characterised by non-cooperation and includes lying down, spitting, hitting out – though relatively gently – and taking his clothes off.

In Chapter 3 we saw that challenging behaviour rarely occurs in a vacuum. There will usually be a reason behind it somewhere. It is likely to be communicating something. In Edward's case, being asked to stop flicking photos and throwing bricks is one thing that can lead to more challenging behaviour, especially if the request to stop comes unexpectedly.

Other reasons behind his challenging behaviour may be harder, even impossible, to pin down, and certainly his behaviour does tend to deteriorate if he is about to have a seizure, but there may be one cause, related indirectly to his epilepsy, which we may be able to address.

Edward's epilepsy is so severe that someone always needs to be near him. That person will be trained in the administration of rescue medication which he or she will carry at all times. This means that in effect Edward is never free of the presence of another person. He is always followed. His whole life has been lived under someone else's watchful eye. This is something we won't be able to change. It's part of his agreed care plan. It is and will always be part of Edward's life.

What we can do, though, is try to understand what it must be like for Edward to be followed and watched 24 hours a day. In a very real way, Edward's life is more restricted, more controlled than most people's. Certainly more so than any of the other students we have met. Perhaps it's not so surprising that when asked to change classrooms, or come to the table for an activity, or for lunch, or to get his coat on, he withdraws his goodwill, lies down, spits, or in extreme circumstances takes his clothes off?

Perhaps we need to let him off the hook a bit, cut him a bit of slack? Allow him to indulge his enthusiasm for flicking photos and throwing bricks a bit longer than usual, and accept that for Edward an activity, a 'lesson', might not always start or finish at the appointed time?

In fact, perhaps Edward is at an age now when the structures and patterns of a conventional lesson or timetable have less meaning. It happens with most 18-year-olds after all. Soon Edward will be moving beyond school. We need to begin exploring what John Carswell in Chapter 7 calls Edward's 'vocation' – not his job, but whatever will give him an active and fulfilling life.

What makes Edward happy?

Being with people he likes, Ramzi and Karl for instance; swimming – he loves that and is very good at it; horse riding and being with horses – that has always been very important for Edward; spending time in the sensory room; being outdoors, moving around, walking, rambling.

His timetable is beginning to take shape.

Throwing things too. We may never fully understand why Edward flicks photos and throws bricks, but what we can do is accept that at least on some level he interprets the world in a 'projectile' way. Ramzi seeks to understand things by putting them in his mouth, Kyle seeks to understand things by humming and singing, and Edward seeks to understand things by throwing them. That's how he is.

Perhaps projectile activities like bowls, cricket, football, magnetic darts, hoop-la or skittles can be part of his curriculum too?

How can Edward be more independent?

That's a tricky one. How can he be independent when there is always someone near him?

First, whoever is carrying Edward's medication needs to understand that they are part of Edward's world and, without compromising his safety, allow him a bit of space. They have to watch him, but not too intrusively; be with him, but not too closely; sit near him, but not always next to him. Allow him to express himself, to be himself, safely.

Beyond that, perhaps the 'no' line for Edward needs to be drawn a little further off? It might sound like indulgence, but in fact it is just giving him the time and space to explore, to experiment. To feel independent.

As his dad tells us, Edward loves Coca Cola. He has always loved it. There's nothing atypical about that for an 18-year-old. And in any case he rarely drinks a whole bottle. He likes the colour, the fizz of the cap as it comes off, the play of light against the liquid. He likes holding it in his mouth and slowly letting it dribble back into the bottle. Not particularly pleasant, but harmless.

In a shop or a supermarket or at the swimming pool he will usually go straight to the display of soft drinks. If we try to steer him away, his behaviour may rapidly deteriorate. But that isn't a reason not to take him out in the community.

Displays of soft drinks are, after all, designed to be appealing to young people. In many ways, Edward is only actually behaving in a way the marketing people are expecting him to behave. He is being drawn towards the display.

So perhaps we need to let him stay there for a while, just looking. It may not be appropriate for him to have a bottle of Coke at this point. He may have one later, or not at all. But it may also be easier for him to leave the shop when he is ready, when everyone else is leaving, when he feels like going back to school. Like Karl finally getting out of the car, it may take a while, but he will have made his own decision. Autonomously.

Similarly, Edward doesn't always want to eat his lunch at the appointed time. It's not surprising really. His seizures often affect his sleep patterns. Sometimes he is awake most of the night. After a seizure he often sleeps for hours during the day. His life doesn't follow a regulated pattern, and he might not always be ready for his meals at the same time as the people around him.

Meal times are often characterised by lack of cooperation, but that might simply be because Edward isn't ready to eat. He is 18, and we need to be prepared to allow him that freedom.

If we allow Edward these small freedoms, these small tastes of autonomy, it could also be that in time he will cooperate more when it comes to taking part in a class activity. He may, generally, be more relaxed, less anxious, more willing to sit at a table with a friend or member of staff and try out a more conventional classroom activity. We will have taken the long route to get to this point, but for Edward it might have been a more meaningful and less stressful route. His route.

How can we help Edward communicate a little more?

Edward actually communicates quite clearly about a lot of things already. He can shake and nod his head, he can say 'hello' and 'no', he can take himself off to the toilet, he can lead people to something he wants, he can point very accurately, he can get a lot of things himself, he can sign 'please and thank you' as well as 'sorry'. He can show love and affection, and displeasure using sounds and gestures.

That's a pretty good repertoire. He doesn't use picture- or symbol-based systems very well right now, not necessarily because he doesn't understand the concept, but probably because it is far more fun for him to flick them across the room, or post them through a window.

The kind of communication he needs right now may be just the feeling of someone being there for him, being responsive to his needs, accepting him, looking through photos with him, using bricks with him. Just letting him know it is OK to be Edward.

The environment around Edward

What Edward needs is space. To feel he has space and options and choices. He needs to feel he owns the space around him, that it is his, even if he is sharing it with Ramzi, and Alice, and Usha and all the others. Whoever is holding his medication needs to respect that and allow him to lead, to show, to explore.

His timetable will need to have variety. It will be all too easy to restrict Edward to one room, where we know his seizures can be dealt with easily, but that is not something which Edward himself will benefit from. He needs real experiences: a swimming pool, a shopping centre, a boat, a climbing wall, a canoe. The staff team will need to be trained and ready to deal with a seizure in any of these places.

So what might some of Edward's targets look like? Here are some suggestions which address some of the issues we have talked about in this chapter:

- *To take part for increasing lengths of time in the classroom routine.* He may be nearly old enough to leave school, but groups and routines are part of life and although we need to respect his need for autonomy, we must also make sure he can still be a member of different social groups.

- *To eat one meal a day at the table.* Some targets for young people with complex needs are also targets, or at least nudges, for staff. In a hectic class environment, it's easy to rush Edward through a meal. Feed him even. This is doing no one any good, least of all Edward. No matter what the time, it will always be worth waiting for Edward to be ready to come to the table and eat. It's an important skill for life.

- *To take part in at least one physical activity every day.* Swimming, horse riding, a walk in the park. Whatever the weather.

- *To have at least one hour of 'Edward Time' every day.* A time for Edward to choose, to lead, to set the agenda. To take his carer with him wherever he wants to go. To be independent, and safe.

- *To explore a new sensory stimulus every day.* Edward knows what he likes – photos and bricks for instance – but his parents want him to broaden his horizons. This doesn't have to be on the scale of a new roller-coaster ride, it might just be for him to touch, or taste or hear something new every day.

Let's leave the last word in this book to Edward's dad as he reflects on the last 18 years. His words say a great deal about accepting and valuing a young person with complex needs:

> *Life certainly hasn't been boring! I have got a few more grey hairs than I would have had, a few more lines on my face. Perhaps I would have sat on the sofa more and drunk more beer, I don't know, because you don't have parallel lives do you? You have one life and do it in a certain way to the best of your ability. We've been dealt these particular cards and we have had to cope with it. I think that it has certainly given us a broader outlook on our lives. We love him enormously, that's the one thing and we wouldn't change it. We wouldn't say, 'Oh, we wish it never happened, oh, we wish we never had Edward.' He has still enriched our lives.*

References

About Learning Disabilities (2012) See www.aboutlearningdisabilities.co.uk, accessed on 21 January 2013.

Australian Institute of Health and Welfare (2008) See www.aihw.gov.au, accessed on 21 January 2013.

Department for Education (2012) *Children with Special Educational Needs: an analysis 2012*. Table 1.4: Maintained primary, state funded secondary and special schools: Number and percentage of pupils by type of need. London: SFR24.

Department of Health (2001) *Valuing people: a new strategy for learning disability for the 21st century*. White Paper. London: DoH. Available at www.dh.gov.uk/en/Publicationsandstatistics/Publications/PublicationsPolicyAndGuidance/DH_4009153, accessed on 21 January 2013.

Douglas Silas Solicitors (2012) See www.specialeducationalneeds.co.uk, accessed on 21 January 2013.

Education Review Office, New Zealand (2013) See www.ero.govt.nz, accessed on 21 January 2013.

Imray, P. (2005) Moving towards simple, understandable and workable definitions of SLD and PMLD. *The SLD Experience 42*, 33–37.

Imray, P. (2011) See www.lists.education.gov.uk/mailman/listinfo/sld-forum, accessed on 21 January 2013. The SLD Forum is an online discussion group hosted by the UK Department for Education for professionals involved in the education of learners with severe, profound and multiple learning difficulties.

Office for Standards in Education (2012a) *The Framework for School Inspection*. London: Ofsted. Available at www.ofsted.gov.uk/resources/framework-for-school-inspection, accessed on 21 January 2013.

Office for Standards in Education (2012b) *School Inspection Handbook*. London: Ofsted. Available at www.ofsted.gov.uk/resources/school-inspection-handbook, accessed on 21 January 2013.

Office for Standards in Education (2013) *Subsidiary guidance supporting the inspection of maintained schools and academies*. London: Ofsted. Available at www.ofsted.gov.uk/resources/subsidiary-guidance-supporting-inspection-of-maintained-schools-and-academies, accessed on 27 March 2013.

PMLD and Mencap (2004) See www.pmldnetwork.org and www.mencap.org.uk, accessed on 21 January 2013. The PMLD Network Forum is an online forum chaired by Mencap where current issues are debated and where individuals can post details of the barriers they are facing and get advice and support.

QCA (2009) *Learning difficulties: Planning, teaching and assessing the curriculum.* Available at http://collections.europarchive.org/tna/20061003092949/qca.org.uk/qca_11583.aspx, accessed on 21 January 2013.

QCDA (2007) *Personalising the curriculum for 14–25s with learning difficulties.*

Available at http://collections.europarchive.org/tna/20061003092949/http://qca.org.uk/qca_13985.aspx, accessed on 21 January 2013. The UK Qualifications and Curriculum Development Agency (QCDA) was the non-regulatory part of the Qualifications and Curriculum Authority (QCA) before its closure in March 2012.

US National Center for Educational Statistics (2008/09) See www.nces.ed.gov, accessed on 21 January 2013.

For further information go to www.andrewcolley.com.

Index

Aaron
 independence of 89
 targets for 121
About Learning Disabilities 21
Alfie
 communication skills 85–6
 and friendships 80
 learning experiences 99
 targets for 121
Alice
 assessment of 46, 51
 behaviour of 53
 communication skills 85
 curriculum for 69–70
 in 'girls group' 98
 introduction to 17
 learning experiences 77, 104
 and music 102
 targets for 116, 123–4
 timetable for 113
Angelman syndrome 35
assessments
 dialogue phase 40–6
 evidence for 127–32
 observation and interaction phase 46–52
 of pupil progress 124–6
 research phase 34–40
assistive technologies 102–3
augmentative or alternative communication
  systems (AAC) 84–6
Australian Institute of Health and Welfare 26
autism 35–6

Barbrook, Jane
 on targets 120
 on transferable skills 73
Baxter, Gail
 on décor in schools 103
 on school integration 96
 on school resources 105

behaviour
 and bribery 60–1
 "challenging" 56–61
 descriptions of different kinds 53–6
 extreme 61–5
 in school 64–5
 sexualised 67
 spitting 66–7
 strategies for 59–61, 64–5
 in supermarkets 55–6
Ben
 assessment of 46, 48, 50
 behaviour of 53, 63
 communication skills 82
 exercise 92
 and friendships 80
 independence of 89–90, 91
 introduction to 16
 learning experiences 99
 and music 102
 targets for 116, 120
 timetable for 110, 113
bribery 60–1
Bridge School, Islington 22

Calow, Lucie
 on school inspections 130–1
 on targets 126
 on transferable skills 74
Carswell, John
 and assessment 127
 and transition from school 135
cerebral palsy 36
"challenging" behaviour 56–61
Chelmsford College, Essex
 transition from school programme 135,
   136–41
communication skills 81–7, 158
craniosynotosis 36
curriculum-based teaching 69–70, 110–13,
   154–6

Daniel
    assessment of 50
    behaviour of 53, 62–4
    communication skills 82
    exercise 92
    and friendships 80
    independence of 87–8
    integration in school 97–8
    introduction to 15
    learning experiences 71, 80, 100
    need for space 100
    teaching 68, 69
    timetable for 110, 113
décor in schools 103–5
Department of Health 26
dialogue phase of assessment 40–6
Douglas Silas Solicitors 20
Down's syndrome 36–7
Duchenne muscular dystrophy 37

Edith Borthwick School, Essex 134
Edward
    communication skills 86, 158
    curriculum for 154–6
    and friendships 81, 156
    independence of 156–8
    interview with father about 145–54, 160
    need for space 158–9
    targets for 121, 159–60
evidence for assessments 127–32
exercise 92–3
experiential targets 121–4
extreme behaviours 61–5

formal targets 117–18
friendships 80–1, 156
furniture 101–2

'girls group' 98
global developmental delay 37
Granta School, Cambridgeshire 74
groupings in school 98–100

happiness 79–81
Hillside Special School, Suffolk 96, 103, 105

Imray, Peter
    on definition of PLSD 22, 25
    on groupings in schools 98–9
independence 87–92, 156–8
informal targets 118–19
inspections of schools 129–32
integration in schools 95–8
Interaction Regional Support Network 82

Karl
    assessment of 48–9
    behaviour of 57–9, 106
Kyle
    assessment of 40, 51, 126
    behaviour of 53, 54
    communication skills 82–3, 86
    independence of 88
    introduction to 18–19
    learning experiences 71, 74, 76
    and music 102
    targets for 114–15, 116

learning
    by experience 70
    guiding principles of 29–31
    leadership in 71
    life skills 71
    making connections 73
    and not learning 71
    restrictions on 71
    tangential 72
    transferable skills 73–5
lessons 78–9
life skills 71
Lockwood, Shelley
    on communication skills 82, 83, 86–7

Maass, Mandy
    on transition from school 134–5
Mary
    communication skills 83–4
    exercise 92
    in 'girls group' 98
    sensory work with 93
    targets for 115–16, 117, 118
Mencap 21

Nadia
    targets for 118–19, 121–2
National Curriculum
    guidelines on teaching 27–8
    and PMLD pupils 23–4
neuronal migration disorders 37
New Zealand 28, 124, 133

observation and interaction phase of
    assessment 46–52
Ofsted inspections 129–32

parents
    and dialogue phase of assessment 42–4
personal care 44–5
PMLD Network 21

Prader-Willi syndrome 37–8
profound egocentrism 22–3
Profound and Multiple Learning Difficulties
    (PLSD)
    'baby-like' definition of 24–5
    difficulties of definition of 19–22
    educational definitions 23–4
    and profound egocentrism 22–3
    statistics on 25–6

Qualifications and Curriculum Authority
    (QCA) 24, 28, 125–6
Qualifications and Curriculum Development
    Agency (QCDA) 28, 125–6

Ramzi
    assessment of 40, 46, 50–1, 125
    behaviour of 66–7, 131
    communication skills 82–3
    exercise 92
    and friendships 80, 81
    independence of 87
    introduction to 16–17
    learning experiences 73, 80, 99
    targets for 116, 117, 118, 120
    timetable for 113
resources in schools 104–5
research phase of assessment 34–40
Rett syndrome 38

Sammy
    assessment of 45–6, 51
    behaviour of 53, 54–5
    communication skills 83, 85
    independence of 87
    introduction to 18
    learning experiences 72, 78, 100
    and music 102
    targets for 116
    transition from school 142–4
schools
    assistive technologies in 102–3
    décor in 103–5
    furniture in 101–2
    groupings in 98–100
    inspections of 129–32
    integration in 95–8
    resources in 104–5
    space in 100–2, 158–9
    staff in 106–7
    timetables in 107–13
sensory work 93–4
sexualised behaviour 67

Soanes, Kirsty
    on resources in school 102–3
space in schools 100–2, 158–9
spitting 66–7
staff in schools 106–7
subject-specific targets 120
supermarkets 55–6

tangential learning 72
targets
    examples of 114–17, 159–60
    experiential 121–4
    formal 117–18
    informal 118–19
    as stepping-stones 120
    subject-specific 120
teaching
    communication skills 81–7, 158
    curriculum-based 69–70, 110–13
    exercise 92–3
    experiences of 76–7
    guiding principles of 29–31
    happiness 79–81
    independence 87–92, 156–8
    international comparisons 28
    and lessons 78–9
    and National Curriculum 27–8
    sensory work 93–4
    timetables 107–13
transition from school
    at Chelmsford College, Essex 135, 136–41
    different experiences of 133–5
    and Edward 153–4
    and Sammy 142–4
transferable skills 73–5

United States 26, 28, 124, 133
US National Center for Education Statistics 26
Usha
    assessment of 40, 41–2, 51
    behaviour of 53, 54
    exercise 92
    in 'girls group' 98
    independence of 90
    introduction to 17–18
    learning experiences 74, 99
    targets for 115–16, 117, 118, 123

Valuing People (DoH) 26

Ward, Ros
    on school staff 106
Worster-Drought syndrome 38